The EQUIP

Implementation Guide

Youth to Think and Act Responsibly through a Peer-Helping Approach

Granville Bud Potter

John C. Gibbs

Arnold P. Goldstein

T 76190

Research Press   2612 North Mattis Avenue   Champaign, Illinois 61822   www.researchpress.com

Copyright © 2001 by Granville Bud Potter, John C. Gibbs, and Arnold P. Goldstein

All rights reserved.

Printed in the United States of America.

5   4   3   2   1   01   02   03   04   05

George's Problem Situation: From *Dilemmas for Applied Use,* by A. Colby & B. Speicher, 1973, unpublished manuscript, Harvard University, Cambridge, MA. Copyright 1973 by the authors. Adapted by permission.

Mark's, Alonzo's, and Dave's Problem Situations: From *An Analysis of Social Behavioral Skill Deficits in Delinquent and Nondelinquent Adolescent Boys,* by B. J. Freedman, 1974, unpublished doctoral dissertation, University of Wisconsin, Madison. Copyright 1974 by the author. Adapted by permission.

Leon's and Reggie's Problem Situations: From *Moral Dilemmas at Scioto Village,* by D. W. Meyers, 1982, unpublished manuscript, Ohio Department of Youth Services, Columbus. Copyright 1982 by the author. Adapted by permission.

Juan's Problem Situation: From *Dilemma Session Intervention with Adult Female Offenders: Behavioral and Attitudinal Correlates,* by H. H. Ahlborn, 1986, unpublished manuscript, Ohio Department of Rehabilitation and Correction, Columbus. Copyright 1986 by the author. Adapted by permission.

Handouts and other forms included in this guide may be reproduced for noncommercial use by the original purchaser only, not to extend to reproduction by other parties. Excerpts may be printed in connection with published reviews in periodicals without express permission. No other part of this guide may be reproduced by any means without the written permission of the publisher.

Copies of this book may be ordered from Research Press at the address given on the title page.

Composition by Jeff Helgesen

Printed by McNaughton & Gunn

ISBN 0-87822-460-2

Library of Congress Catalog Number 00-109591

Related materials available from Research Press:

The EQUIP Program: Teaching Youth to Think and Act Responsibly through a Peer-Helping Approach, by John C. Gibbs, Granville Bud Potter, and Arnold P. Goldstein

EQUIPPED for Life (game), by Mary Horn, Randy Shively, and John C. Gibbs

How I Think (HIT) Questionnaire, by John C. Gibbs, Alvaro Q. Barriga, and Granville Bud Potter.

How I Think (HIT) Questionnaire Manual, by Alvaro Q. Barriga, John C. Gibbs, Granville Bud Potter, and Albert K. Liau

Contents

Section 6: Social Skills Training   77

Section 7: Social Decision Making 105

Final Equipment Meeting: Up or Down?   127

Acknowledgments

Some of the new materials included in this guide have been adapted from products generated by Dr. Albert K. Liau (Kent State University) and the staffs at the Alvis House in Columbus, Ohio; the Lubbock County Youth Center of Lubbock, Texas; and the Youth Diagnostic and Development Center in Albuquerque, New Mexico (especially those by Jeff Clements and Suely Porter). We are sure you will appreciate their creative additions to the EQUIP program. The Lubbock County Youth Center contributions (by Angie Alspaugh, Richard Dean, and others) are found mainly in the anger management pages. Finally, we wish to thank all those practitioners who have enlightened us by asking questions and suggesting better ways of applying the "tools of the trade."

Welcome to the EQUIP
Program Implementation Guide

When we (John Gibbs and Bud Potter) do our workshops around the country, many practitioners—teachers, social workers, counselors, psychologists, and administrators—compliment us on our book *The EQUIP Program: Teaching Youth to Think and Act Responsibly through a Peer-Helping Approach* (Gibbs, Potter, & Goldstein, 1995). Nonetheless, many of these colleagues voice a complaint similar to the one expressed by Melanie Dearing and Patty White, our teacher friends in Missouri and Florida, respectively. Melanie and Patty, both busy educators, told us that to run the EQUIP program they needed step-by-step guidance, as well as ready-to-use forms and materials. Furthermore, various busy administrators have expressed the need to know the steps in getting an EQUIP program up and running. This guide is our response to the needs of busy practitioners. We hope that the materials here will lessen your load and give you all the materials you need to initiate and run an effective program.

We need to stress that this guide is not a substitute for the EQUIP book. Although the materials in this guide are "cutting edge" (that is, they are the latest versions, some not even in the book), they are still just the materials. To get a full understanding of what the program is all about, you must start with *The EQUIP Program* and consult it frequently for conceptual guidance as your program develops. To make sure your understanding from the text captures the key points of the EQUIP program, however, we next provide a brief overview.

OVERVIEW OF THE EQUIP PROGRAM

EQUIP is a multicomponent program that starts with formal individualized assessments to facilitate the development of an Individual Performance Plan. EQUIP then combines peer-helping group methods with cognitive development and skills-training approaches designed specifically to motivate and teach youth who have behaved antisocially to think and act responsibly. It emphasizes the positive potential of the targeted youth while recognizing their "3-D" limitations (cognitive *distortions*, social skill *deficiencies*, and sociomoral developmental *delays*). It stresses holding youths accountable for their behavior. By insisting on accountability, we are respecting youths and believing in them as people capable of remedying their limitations—in other words, believing in their positive potential.

EQUIP's basic components—mutual help and teaching—depend on each other. As explained in *The EQUIP Program*, "mutual help" programs need built-in psychoeducation because even the best-motivated youths can't effectively help their peers unless their helping-skill limitations are remedied. Conversely, to be effective, psychoeducational programs need youths to be seriously motivated to change—the great strength of peer helping programs. Recognizing these complementary needs and combining these components create a synergistic "sum," the EQUIP program, that surpasses its parts.

Mutual Help Meetings

In the EQUIP program, mutual help groups of 6 to 9 youths meet daily (for 5 days) for 1 to 1-1/2 hours at a time in adult-coached but youth-run mutual help meetings. Through these meetings, group members help one another think and act responsibly by cultivating a prosocial climate, telling their life stories, reporting and discussing their problems and thinking errors, redirecting negative members, and helping group members plan for release/discharge.

Equipment Meetings

Once the motivational positive peer culture is established, adult-run equipment meetings are typically offered for up to 2 days each week in place of two of the mutual help meetings. The equipment meetings are essential to develop group members' ability to help one another. Specifically, these meetings "equip" participants with anger management techniques (including correction of thinking errors), social skills (remedying social skills deficiencies), and development of mature social decision making concepts and skills (moral education/moral development).

Curriculum Administration

How long does it take to present the EQUIP curriculum through the equipment meetings, and how often is the curriculum presented? Usually, teaching the psychoeducational curriculum (i.e., anger management/correcting thinking errors, social skills training, and social decision making) takes at least 10 weeks. In most schools and agencies, the mutual help meetings are ongoing. The equipment curriculum is repeated periodically so the positive peer culture's helping process remains effective. Ongoing groups can accommodate the open enrollment practices of most schools and other facilities in residential and nonresidential settings. A nice dividend of these ongoing groups is their tendency to foster the positive peer culture of the school or facility at large.

Positive Staff Culture

It is important for the entire staff of the school, day treatment center, institution, etc., to model an effective and positive staff culture if they expect their clientele to achieve an effective and positive peer culture. Each setting for EQUIP implementation must develop a clear, comprehensive program statement, including the requirement that all staff members practice participatory management and teamwork and strive to achieve positive interpersonal interactions.

OVERVIEW OF MATERIALS IN THE GUIDE

All staff members involved in presenting an EQUIP program should study both our original EQUIP book and the corresponding materials presented in this guide. Some of these materials are for use by administrators and staff and some are for use by the young people (whom we refer to as participants or group members). Within each section, the materials are arranged in the suggested order of use for administrators, staff, and youth.

Section One: Implementation Materials

This section briefly describes the steps the administrator should take in setting up for a successful program. The section includes three fill-in-the-blanks forms for the program administrator: Basic Program Requirements Checklist, Comprehensive Program Statement Outline, and List of Operating Procedures. You will find this section helpful whether you are beginning a new program or fine-tuning an existing one.

Section Two: Assessment and Individual Performance Plan

In conducting workshops, we discovered a widespread need for assessing participant progress throughout the program. In this section (as in *The EQUIP Program*), we identify the three social-cognitive or cognitive-behavioral measures we ourselves have found most useful: The *How I Think (HIT) Questionnaire* (Gibbs, Barriga, & Potter, 2001), the *Inventory of Adolescent Problems–Short Form* (IAP–SF; Gibbs, Swillinger et al., 1992, included in Gibbs, Potter, & Goldstein, 1995), and the *Sociomoral Reflection Measure–Short Form* (SRM–SF; Gibbs, Basinger, & Fuller, 1992). Availability information is provided for each of these measures; also included is the Individual Performance Plan, the basic operating agreement among the youth, staff, and family.

Section Three: Mutual Help Meetings

The introductory comments in this section speak to the difficulty of working with resistant, antisocial youth and about how mutual help meetings reduce that resistance—in other words, how they motivate change. Included are several new handouts you (the "coach") can use with participants as you explain the mutual help meeting format and content, and work to develop the common language of the program. Information on the release/discharge meeting is new. Also new are the Coach's Mutual Help Meeting Overview and the Observer's Report and Critique of Mutual Help Meetings. These forms will be particularly helpful to new coaches and to those who are training them.

Section Four: Equipment Meetings

The introductory comments to this section briefly explain the importance and role of the equipment meetings. After the introduction, we present a chart entitled "The Equipment Meeting Curriculum in a Nutshell." The chart shows the order in which the anger management/thinking errors correction, social skills, and social decision making materials are presented across as many as 31 equipment meetings.

Section Five: Anger Management/Thinking Error Correction Meetings

This section provides Equipper's Guidelines for each of the anger management sessions. These guidelines present each session in a step-by-step fashion for easy reference during the anger management/thinking error correction meetings. Some of these guidelines include examples of what the equipper might write on an easel pad or chalkboard. Also included, by session, are participant's handouts, all ready to be reproduced and distributed.

Section Six: Social Skills Training Meetings

We introduce this section by defining social skills and explaining their contribution to effective mutual helping. The format of the social skills training meeting is outlined for ready reference. You will also find the Social Skills Role-Playing Participant's Handout, an introduction to the topic for distribution to group members. A page of Equipper Guidelines and a corresponding Participant Handout are included for each of the 10 social skills presented. Participant Handouts give the title of the social skill, list the steps for group members to follow when practicing the skill, and suggest situations in which participants could use the skill.

Section Seven: Social Decision Making Meetings

This section's introductory comments describe the rationale for the social decision making meetings and include an outline of meeting format and a summary of the stages of moral development. Equipper's Guidelines, including sample probe questions, are provided for the Martian's Adviser's Problem Situation. Page references from *The EQUIP Program* are listed for easy reference to the leader notes on each problem situation.

Because social decision making meetings are usually rather free flowing (i.e., the equipper must adjust his or her comments extensively during the course of the meeting), guidelines for the other nine problem situations are not provided. The section includes a ready-to-reproduce Participant Handout for each of the problem situations.

SECTION ONE
Implementation Materials

INTRODUCTION

The most successful programs have a formal written administrative and programmatic base from which to operate. The forms presented here cover the basic (minimal) administrative issues you must address before launching the EQUIP program—or indeed any program. We have not included legally mandated standards of compliance. We strongly recommend that you comply with all regulatory statutes plus review and consider adopting the standards of a professional accreditation organization.

As Maslow emphasized decades ago, basic human needs for health, security, belonging, and so forth are essential conditions for human development. As applied to the EQUIP program, that means your program must be housed within an environment that is clean, safe, humane, and supportive of positive social interactions for the young people *and* the staff. It is your responsibility to establish and continually monitor this positive environment.

ACTIVITIES AND MATERIALS

To implement and fine-tune the EQUIP program, administrators should do as follows:

1. Read the entire EQUIP book. Chapters 1, 6, 7, and 8 are the most important.

2. Complete the Basic Program Requirements Checklist. If an area on the list needs to be addressed, develop a related action plan and implement it.

3. Study and complete the Comprehensive Program Statement Outline. This form suggests the process for developing the program statement, central to the success of your efforts. It may also be used as a tool to gather program-related suggestions from other staff members.

4. Complete and follow the List of Operating Procedures. This form includes categories that must be addressed, through written policy and procedure, for the program to be successful. Use this form to create a comprehensive set of procedures and to collect staff thoughts about needed procedures or modifications of current procedures.

Basic Program Requirements Checklist

Completed by _____ Date _____

This form applies to both residential and nonresidential settings.

1. Are there policy and supporting procedures that ensure a clean, safe, and humane environment for the program participants, youth and staff alike? ☐ yes ☐ no

2. Has the agency mission statement been clearly articulated and conveyed to the staff? ☐ yes ☐ no
   a. Can the staff repeat it without hesitation? ☐ yes ☐ no
   b. Does their work with the client(s) reflect the mission? ☐ yes ☐ no

3. Has a comprehensive program statement been written and conveyed to the staff? If so, does it include: ☐ yes ☐ no
   a. Characterization of the client population? ☐ yes ☐ no
   b. Overview of the program? ☐ yes ☐ no
   c. Expectations for staff? ☐ yes ☐ no
   d. Program description? ☐ yes ☐ no

4. Have basic directives related to safety, security, and youth behaviors been written and routinized through training, practice, and enforcement? ☐ yes ☐ no

5. Has the *entire* staff been trained in the EQUIP program? ☐ yes ☐ no

6. Do individual staff performance evaluations reflect that person's support for and practice of each component of the program? ☐ yes ☐ no

7. Are the administrative/supervisory staff, on all shifts, held to a high level of program support and practice? ☐ yes ☐ no
   a. Is program compliance a routine item on each administrative/supervisory meeting agenda? ☐ yes ☐ no
   b. If routine reports (monthly, quarterly, etc.) are required, is program support and practice a required reporting item? ☐ yes ☐ no

8. Are staff organized into multidisciplinary, nonhierarchical teams? ☐ yes ☐ no
   a. Is there a directive stating the purpose and operations of the team? ☐ yes ☐ no
   b. Do teams meet once per week for a minimum of 75 minutes? ☐ yes ☐ no

9. Have staff members received training on appropriate interpersonal behaviors, and are staff expected to practice these behaviors at all times? ☐ yes ☐ no

10. Is there a program integrity (quality assurance) system in place? ☐ yes ☐ no
    a. Are operational standards in place and regularly reviewed for compliance? ☐ yes ☐ no
    b. Are coaches and equippers routinely observed and critiqued by one another and/or knowledgeable trainers? ☐ yes ☐ no
    c. Are treatment teams routinely observed and critiqued by knowledgeable practitioners? ☐ yes ☐ no
    d. Is there a program evaluation plan in place? ☐ yes ☐ no

11. Do most of the clients who complete the program view their participation as a positive experience? ☐ yes ☐ no

Comprehensive Program Statement Outline

Completed by _____ Date _____

Include attachments as needed.

Mission statement

Write a paragraph that succinctly presents the purpose of the agency/program.

_____

_____

_____

_____

_____

Guiding principles

List the underlying values, beliefs, and concepts that define the program content and delivery. (You may need to expand the list to more than the number available here.)

1. _____

_____

2. _____

_____

3. _____

_____

4. _____

_____

5. _____

_____

Program overview

List and briefly describe all of the curricular components. The listed areas should eventually have formal, comprehensive descriptions with related operational procedures readily available for staff reference.

Population description

_____

_____

_____

_____

Nature and expectations of staff

_____

_____

_____

_____

Client assessment and planning

_____
_____
_____
_____

Education (list all areas and levels)

_____
_____
_____
_____

Counseling (individual, group, methods)

_____
_____
_____
_____

Community service

_____
_____
_____
_____

Aftercare

_____
_____
_____
_____

Other components (spiritual, recreational, extracurricular, levels, awards, etc.)

_____
_____
_____
_____

Summary statement
Give a capsule description of the program, its philosophy, hopes for the future, etc.

_____
_____
_____
_____

List of Operating Procedures

Completed by _____ Date _____

List all of the procedures required to ensure appropriate levels of safety, security, and program delivery. You may need to extend your list beyond these examples to meet all of your legal and voluntary requirements.

Administration and supervision (management responsibilities, leadership, etc.)

_____

_____

_____

_____

Facility maintenance and sanitation

_____

_____

_____

_____

Safety, security, and emergency procedures

_____

_____

_____

_____

Population enrollment/admission/transfers/releases (who, how, orientation, etc.)

_____

_____

_____

_____

Health care (pre-enrollment requirements, screening, ongoing care, etc.)

_____

_____

_____

_____

Student assessment and planning (assessments used, individual plans, review process, etc.)

_____

_____

_____

_____

Population records (management, confidentiality, etc.)

_____

_____

_____

_____

Behavior management (rules and potential consequences, level system, grievance system, etc.)

_____

_____

_____

_____

Staff teams (purpose, membership, meetings and agendas, responsibilities, etc.)

_____

_____

_____

_____

Program delivery (curriculum statements and revisions, schedules, reports, etc.)

_____

_____

_____

_____

Staff development and training (preservice training, lesson plan format, etc.)

_____

_____

_____

_____

Quality assurance (standards, review process, program evaluation/research, etc.)

_____

_____

_____

_____

Other (budgets, personnel, program visitors, transportation, etc.)

_____

_____

_____

_____

SECTION TWO

Assessment and Individual Performance Plan

INTRODUCTION

We have been asked on many occasions, "How do we know what a group member should be working on?" We share that, after listening to a life story (described in section 3), the group assigns thinking errors and problems for the group member to work on. The staff and family members also offer their observations and suggest areas for improvement.

We generally recommend the use of psychometrically developed assessment instruments. The recommended areas for assessment are medical, psychological, educational, and vocational. Many such instruments are available, depending upon the age and needs of the population you serve. If you are in the criminal justice field, we strongly recommend the use of locally validated risk assessments. The National Institute of Corrections and the Centers for Disease Control and Prevention (Division of Violence Prevention) can provide you with up-to-date information (see, for example, the CDC's compendium *Measuring Violence-Related Attitudes, Beliefs, and Behaviors among Youths* [Dahlberg, Toal, & Behrens, 1998] on the use of various risk and progress assessment tools).

Psychological assessments should include measures of participants' progress in the three areas corresponding to the EQUIP curriculum: reducing self-serving cognitive distortions (anger management/thinking error correction), enhancing skills for constructive social interaction (social skills training), and facilitating maturity of moral judgment (social decision making). Measures we have found most helpful in these areas are, respectively:

- *How I Think (HIT) Questionnaire* (Gibbs, Barriga, & Potter, 2001). The HIT Questionnaire is available, along with the *How I Think (HIT) Questionnaire Manual* (Barriga, Gibbs, Potter, & Liau, 2001), from Research Press at the address given on the title page of this guide.

- *Inventory of Adolescent Problems–Short Form* (IAP–SF; Gibbs, Swillinger et al., 1992, included in Gibbs, Potter, and Goldstein, 1995). The IAP–SF is given as Appendix B in the EQUIP book (Gibbs et al., 1995).

- *Sociomoral Reflection Measure–Short Form* (SRM–SF). The Social Reflection Questionnaire of the SRM–SF appears as Appendix A of the EQUIP book. A rating form, scoring manual, and self-training materials for the questionnaire are included in *Moral Maturity: Measuring the Development of Sociomoral Reflection* (pp. 149–153), by J. C. Gibbs, K. S. Basinger, and D. Fuller, 1992 (Hillsdale, NJ: Erlbaum).

ACTIVITIES AND MATERIALS

Included in this section is the individual performance plan, a simple, workable, and nonbureaucratic form that serves as the basic operating agreement and contract among the youth, the staff, and the family. The participant should complete this document before he or she is enrolled in the mutual help and equipment group meetings. We also advise a review of other, more comprehensive documents that delineate the results of formal and informal assessments, and corresponding goals and objectives. For example, a participant may have an individualized education program (IEP) plan. Other participants may have probation or parole plans that include sophisticated service and supervision requirements. Some programs may require that the performance plan be reviewed and updated periodically.

Individual Performance Plan

Participant name _____ Date _____

My Individual Performance Plan is based on personal information and a battery of needs assessments that I did/will do my best to complete in an accurate and truthful way. The goals stated here were created as a result of the needs assessment and through discussion and negotiation with staff and family members.

My strengths are (artistic, athletic, academic, hard worker, articulate, etc.)

1. _____
2. _____
3. _____
4. _____
5. _____

General goals

Initial each to show that you agree.

_____ 1. I will accept the responsibility of behaving in a positive manner at all times. This includes completing assignments and being an active participant in all required meetings, classes, and other activities.

_____ 2. I will help others and myself.

_____ 3. I will accept direction from the staff and other authority figures.

_____ 4. I will develop an understanding of my thoughts, feelings, and actions and how they can be harmful or helpful to others or myself.

_____ 5. I will accept responsibility for my irresponsible behavior and the harm it has done to others.

_____ 6. I will develop and use action plans to correct the harm I have caused or may cause to others.

_____ 7. I will demonstrate being a responsible person by managing my anger, using constructive social skills, and treating others as I hope that they would treat me.

_____ 8. I will follow the rules of the agency and the community.

My individual thinking and behavior goals

1. To identify, own, and correct my thinking errors. (List them in order of importance to you.)

   a. Self-Centered

   I use the following thinking errors to justify my Self-Centered thinking: Minimizing/Mislabeling, Blaming Others, and Assuming the Worst.

   b. _____

   c. _____

   d. _____

2. To identify, own, and correct my social/behavioral problems. (Number your four most serious problems from 1–4.)

____ a. Low Self-Image	____ g. Misleads Others
____ b. Inconsiderate of Self	____ h. Easily Misled
____ c. Inconsiderate of Others	____ i. Alcohol or Drug Problem
____ d. Authority Problem	____ j. Stealing
____ e. Easily Angered	____ k. Lying
____ f. Aggravates Others	____ l. Fronting

My educational goals are

1. To graduate from high school or get a G.E.D. in _____, 20___

2. Other _____

My employment goals

1. Short term _____

2. Long term _____

My other goals

1. Short term _____

2. Short term _____

3. Long term _____

4. Long term _____

By completing and signing this document, I agree to fulfill the identified goals to the best of my ability. I also agree that the goals cannot all be fulfilled while in this program and will require my continued efforts even after my graduation, release, or transfer from this program. If I fail to fulfill my obligations, I agree to accept the consequences for my behavior.

Participant

Signature _____ Date _____

Staff and family

By signing this document we agree to assist _____ in the fulfillment of

his/her goals. Our approach will always be positive and supportive. This may include admitting that we

made a mistake, apologizing for that mistake, and, to the best of our ability, correcting the harm done. It

may also include holding _____ responsible for his/her behavior and meting

out or supporting appropriate disciplinary action(s).

Signature for staff _____ Date _____

Signature for family _____ Date _____

SECTION THREE
Mutual Help Meetings

INTRODUCTION

Like most practitioners, you have probably recognized that young people who have been antisocial often initially lack the motivation to change their patterns of irresponsible thinking and behavior. Even though they have failed at school and might already have experienced the impact of the legal system, they still may not be motivated to change. Sometimes just to escape the disapproval of parents and wrath of authority figures, and to get what they want, they will verbalize regret and a willingness to change their self-centered and harmful behavior. Once away from those figures, however, they may actively resist suggestions that they identify and "own" their thinking errors and problems and replace them with socially acceptable and responsible behavior. They most often take a victim stance (what we call Self-Centered) and justify that stance by blaming others, minimizing or mislabeling their irresponsible behavior, and assuming the worst about others and/or situations.

As the adult responsible for introducing opportunities for change in these areas, it is likely that you all too often suffer these self-centered and resistant youths' verbal and behavioral abuse. We too have faced this frustrating situation. We have found that a positive peer culture, developed and maintained through the use of the mutual help meetings, is the most effective method of motivating young persons to think and act responsibly. It is the positive peer culture that first helps to tap youths' positive potential for prosocial change.

The program staff responsible for leading the youth-run mutual help meetings are called "coaches" because they prompt, encourage, and give feedback to group members in the same way a coach in sports would.

FORMAT OF THE MUTUAL HELP MEETING

The Participant Handout entitled "Parts of the Mutual Help Meeting" gives a concise description of mutual help meeting format. Although the handout is written for group members, coaches will find it a useful reminder for in-meeting use.

ACTIVITIES AND MATERIALS

In preparation for implementing mutual help meetings, coaches should do as follows:

1. Read chapters 1, 2, and 6 of the EQUIP book. The coach must also be familiar with the equipment meeting curriculum; after all, he or she will be responsible for reminding the group to use their "equipment" as they discuss their thinking errors and problem behaviors and as they develop their respective action plans.

2. Work with other staff to establish the right context for the group meetings (see chapters 6 and 7 of the EQUIP text). A meeting between the staff and the youth group must be held before any materials are shared. It may be useful for a staff member (or members) to meet individually with the participant, the family, and anyone else concerned with the youth's welfare (e.g., probation officers) to establish the youth's willingness and commitment to participate in the group process. The parents and/or other adults must be informed of the youth's progress and can help maintain the motivation and commitment to participate.

3. Review the Participant Handouts and decide when to share them with group members. Although it is not mandatory, we suggest that you use these handouts in the order they are given. In a new group, the coach helps participants complete the handouts as they are assigned. Youth entering an ongoing group may need help to complete any handouts the group has already completed. If one of the more senior group members takes on this responsibility, both the new member and the "seasoned" one will benefit.

4. Before each meeting, photocopy enough Participant Handouts so every group member may have one.

The Participant Handouts for the mutual help meetings, new to this guide, are designed to help introduce the process and content of the group, as well as the common language participants will use. Coaches may feel free to present these handouts in any order they wish.

- *Problem Names.* Explains what a "problem" is, as the term is used in the group, and lists and describes three general and nine specific problems. Fill-in-the blanks help participants recognize and apply these problems to their own lives.

- *Thinking Errors.* Defines and labels the four thinking errors and gives examples to illustrate how they are used.

- *Problems and Thinking Errors Daily Log.* A handout for group members to record problems and associated thinking errors. The last section of the log permits the participant to record his or her corrective action plan. The log serves as a record of improvement in patterns of thinking and behavior.

  The Problems and Thinking Errors Daily Log has evolved from the original log presented in the EQUIP book and is somewhat different from that version. In EQUIP, we recommended presenting anger logs in the third session of the anger management/thinking error correction course. However, our more recent experience has convinced us that giving group members the opportunity for this type of self-evaluation earlier on better helps them identify specific problems and thinking errors. We recommend that the log be presented shortly after mutual help meetings begin, if not before. That way, group members may become familiar with and begin using the log informally in mutual help and equipment meetings, as well as in the general program setting. The log is also reproduced in Session 3 of the anger management/thinking error corrections course (see p. 57), along with a structured introduction to its use.

- *Ground Rules.* Presents 13 ground rules for mutual help meetings *and* equipment meetings. The list includes several rules that do not appear in the original EQUIP text. Practitioners have found that the new rules prevent problems by enhancing the group's level of self-control. This handout also serves as a guide for the coach (or equipper) as he or she explains the ground rules for the first time. The coach/equipper should answer the questions on the handout before explaining the ground rules to the group. The participants then answer the questions on the handout to personalize the rules. The handout also helps participants structure their explanation of the ground rules to new group members.

- *Parts of the Mutual Help Meeting.* Outlines and describes the components of the mutual help meeting for the group members. Senior group members may wish to use this handout to help them explain the meeting to new members.

- *Your Turn: Parts of the Mutual Help Meeting.* A blank form that permits group members to summarize the format of the mutual help meeting in their own words.

- *Life Story Meeting.* Explains the purpose of sharing life stories, as well as how and when to tell one. This handout ends with several questions that serve as a content review.

- *My Life Story.* Lists the components of the life story to help group members organize their own stories and use as a reference when telling that story.

For coaches, we include the following forms. The observer's form includes space to record the developmental stage of the group (forming, storming, norming, and positive peer culture). An explanation of these stages appears in the EQUIP book (see p. 22).

- *Coach's Mutual Help Meeting Overview.* Helps the coach before, during, and after the mutual help meeting by giving the coach the opportunity to record pre-meeting notes, document problem and thinking error reporting and group interactions, and record notes during and after the meeting. Completed forms should be kept in a notebook for reference by the regular coach, a substitute coach, the equipper, or any other team member with a need to know.

- *Observer's Report and Critique of Mutual Help Meetings.* Used by someone observing the mutual help meeting(s) for the purpose of providing the coach with constructive feedback. After completing the form, the observer uses it as a guide to critique the coach's performance, then gives the coach a copy of the form or other observer's notes.

THE RELEASE/DISCHARGE MEETING

Whether you are running a residential or nonresidential program, there will come a time when youth must be released or discharged from the group meetings. The release/discharge meeting, a special kind of mutual help meeting like the life story meeting, is an opportunity for the group to have input in the decision without having the responsibility for the final decision. The final decision is the responsibility of the staff team. It has been our experience that new group members take the program much more seriously if they know that they must request a recommendation for discharge/release from their group. Furthermore, the required structured planning and presentation help participants to understand their past and present, and to think and act responsibly as they plan their future. Because the procedures for the release/discharge meeting are new to this guide, we will describe them in some detail.

Purposes of the Release/Discharge Meeting

The release/discharge meeting gives the group member the opportunity to do the following:

1. Provide a thorough review of his/her problems and thinking errors, including the problems and thinking errors assigned based upon the life story.

2. Explain the effect his or her thinking and behavior has had on self and other people.

3. Explain how his or her thinking and behavior have changed, including specific examples of things he or she has done to correct harm done to other people (problem-related action plans).

4. Share how he or she has helped fellow group members (specific examples are required). The group member concerned affirms or clarifies the examples.

5. Share his or her plans for the immediate future and thereafter (education, AA meetings, community service, employment, etc.).

6. Ask the group for a recommendation that he or she receive the release.

7. Ask the group to identify any problems and issues that he or she should continue to work on.

This meeting also gives other group members the chance to help by doing the following:

1. Relating to the youth any problems and issues that he or she should continue to work on (e.g., Easily Misled problem, Assuming the Worst thinking error, use of anger reducers, parenting, etc.).

2. Giving a recommendation to the staff that the youth receive (or not receive) permission for release.

3. Stating the reasons for giving or withholding recommendation for the person's release or transfer.

The group member requests the release/discharge meeting, and the meeting is awarded in the same manner as for the mutual help meeting and the life story meeting. The Participant's Handout for the release/discharge meeting (*Release/Discharge Meeting Questions*) includes a number of questions for the participant to answer in preparing for the meeting.

The group may ask any appropriate question during the meeting. Using "ask, don't tell" and other constructive intervention techniques (see pp. 23–32 of the EQUIP book), the coach prompts the group to ask pertinent questions and ensures that the youth and the group respect the seriousness of the youth's release/discharge. Group members must realize that they are contributing to a decision that may have a profound effect upon that group member's life, as well as on the lives of others. The group must reach a consensus recommendation; the coach then advises the staff team of the group's recommendation.

It is the staff team's responsibility to make the final decision regarding the youth's release or discharge, especially if the agency is serving youth who have broken the law. If participation in the group is voluntary, the staff team may give more weight to the recommendation of the group. Even for voluntary participants, we recommend using an Individual Performance Plan that also serves as a contract between the participant and the staff.

Problem Names

Name _____ Date _____

Read the entire document, then reread each item and follow the instructions.

Social/behavioral problems are actions that cause harm to oneself, others, or property.

1. Has someone else's problem(s) ever hurt you? ☐ yes ☐ no

   Think of a time that someone's problem(s) have hurt you. Choose the best name for that problem from the list below and write it here.

   _____

2. Has your problem ever hurt someone else? ☐ yes ☐ no

   Think of a time your problem hurt someone else. Choose the best name for that problem from the list below and write it here.

   _____

General problems

The first three problems are general problems. These general problems may be related to any of the specific problems. When you use one of the general problem names to describe a behavior, to get a good understanding of the situation you *must* also name one of the specific problems (see the next page).

1. Low Self-Image

The person has a poor opinion of him- or herself. Often feels put down or of little worth. Quits easily. Plays "poor me" or sees him- or herself as the victim even when harming others. Feels accepted only by other people who also feel bad about themselves.

Briefly describe a situation where you or someone you know showed a low self-image problem.

_____

Was a specific problem shown at the same time? ☐ yes ☐ no
What was the problem?

_____

2. Inconsiderate of Self

The person does things that are damaging to him- or herself. He or she tries to run from problems and often denies them.

Briefly describe a situation where you or someone you know showed an Inconsiderate of Self problem.

_____

Was a specific problem shown at the same time? ☐ yes ☐ no
What was the problem?

_____

3. Inconsiderate of Others

The person does things that are harmful to others. Doesn't care about needs or feelings of others. Enjoys putting people down or laughing at them. Takes advantage of weaker people or those with problems.

_____

Briefly describe a situation where you or someone you know showed an Inconsiderate of Others problem.

_____

_____

Was a specific problem shown at the same time? ☐ yes ☐ no
What was the problem?

_____

Specific problems

4. Authority Problem

The person gets into major confrontations with teachers, parents, and others in authority, often over minor matters. Resents anyone telling him or her what to do or even giving advice. Won't listen. Even when complying, glares, sulks, or curses.

I know someone who has this problem.   ☐ yes ☐ no
I have this problem.   ☐ yes ☐ no

5. Easily Angered

The person quickly takes offense, is easily frustrated or irritated; throws tantrums.

I know someone who has this problem.   ☐ yes ☐ no
I have this problem.   ☐ yes ☐ no

6. Aggravates Others

The person threatens, bullies, hassles, teases, or uses put-downs to hurt other people. "Pays back," even when others didn't mean to put the person down.

I know someone who has this problem.   ☐ yes ☐ no
I have this problem.   ☐ yes ☐ no

7. Misleads Others

Manipulates others into doing the dirty work; will abandon that person if the person is caught.

I know someone who has this problem.   ☐ yes ☐ no
I have this problem.   ☐ yes ☐ no

8. Easily Misled

The person prefers to associate with irresponsible peers and is easily drawn into their antisocial behavior. Willing to be their flunky—hopes to gain their approval.

I know someone who has this problem.   ☐ yes ☐ no
I have this problem.   ☐ yes ☐ no

9. Alcohol or Drug Problem

The person misuses substances that hurt him or her, and is afraid of not having friends otherwise. Is afraid to face life without a crutch. Avoids issues and people through substance abuse. Usually is very self-centered and minimizes the use of drugs by saying they are not bad or within his or her control. When the person does something wrong, he or she blames the drugs by saying, "I was high—I couldn't help it."

I know someone who has this problem.   ☐ yes ☐ no
I have this problem.   ☐ yes ☐ no

10. Stealing

The person takes things that belong to others. Doesn't respect others. Is willing to hurt another person to take what he or she wants.

I know someone who has this problem.	☐ yes ☐ no
I have this problem.	☐ yes ☐ no

11. Lying

The person cannot be trusted to tell the truth or the whole story. Twists the truth to create a false impression. Denies everything when he or she thinks it is possible to get away with it. Finds it exciting to scheme and then get away with a lie—in other words, to "get over" on people. May even lie when there is nothing to be gained.

I know someone who has this problem.	☐ yes ☐ no
I have this problem.	☐ yes ☐ no

12. Fronting

The person tries to impress others, puffs him- or herself up, puts on an act. Clowns around to get attention. Is afraid to show his or her true feelings.

I know someone who has this problem.	☐ yes ☐ no
I have this problem.	☐ yes ☐ no

How many problems do you have? _____

What are your most serious problems?

Number 1 problem _____

Number 2 problem _____

Number 3 problem _____

By correctly identifying your problems, you have taken a big step in helping yourself. Save this handout to use later in the program. You may find it very useful.

Thinking Errors

Name _____ Date _____

The following terms are used to identify thinking errors. These terms are used in the group meetings and throughout the program. When you name your behavioral problem, the thinking error that caused it is also named. *Remember: It is your thinking error that leads to your social/behavioral problem.*

The Primary Thinking Error

1. Self-Centered

Self-Centered thinking means that you think your opinions and feelings are more important than the opinions and feelings of other people. You may not even consider how another person might feel about things. Self-Centered thinking can also mean that you think only about what you want right now and do not think about how your behaviors will affect you or others in the future.

Self-Centered is the "primary," or basic, thinking error. The Self-Centered thinking error can severely limit one person's consideration for the viewpoint of another person.

Does someone you know seem to have a Self-Centered thinking error? How do you know? Explain without using the person's name.

_____

_____

_____

It is important to understand that a person's thoughts cannot be known by anyone other than that person. You can guess what a person is thinking, but you will not know for sure until that person shares his or her thoughts.

Has anyone ever said to you, "I know what you are thinking," but then was wrong? Explain.

_____

_____

_____

If you want to know what another person is thinking, what do you have to do?

_____

Secondary Thinking Errors

The Self-Centered person uses other (secondary) thinking errors to avoid feeling bad (guilt, remorse, low self-concept) about his or her bad (antisocial) behavior and to allow the selfish thoughts and behaviors to continue. The Self-Centered person almost always shows his or her basic self-centered thinking error *and* one of the following secondary thinking errors.

2. Minimizing/Mislabeling

Minimizing means that you think your problems or behaviors are not as bad or wrong as they really are. Mislabeling means that you put a label on your wrong or harmful behavior to try to make it OK or good. Minimizing/Mislabeling can also mean that you may call other people bad names so it will seem OK to hurt them.

Examples

- "We just went for a little joyride!" What really happened: "We stole someone's car and rode around for hours, then left the car when it ran out of gas."

- "It really didn't hurt her. I only pushed her." What really happened: "The girl is in pain because I slammed her hard against the wall."

- "He was a snitch and got jumped." What really happened: "I punched and kicked him because he told his neighbor the truth, that I was the person who stole the neighbor's stereo." Or, what really happened: The young man was brutally beaten because he told the principal that someone had a gun and threatened some other kids.

Write another example and explain.

_____

_____

_____

3. Assuming the Worst

Assuming the Worst means that you think that only bad things can happen to you and that you cannot do anything about what happens. It also means that you think that you or other people will not be able to change or make improvements. Assuming the Worst can also mean that you think that others are always selfish or out to get you or someone else.

Examples

- A guy bumped into you and your friend. You think that he did it on purpose instead of thinking it was an accident. What really happened: Everyone was late and rushing to get to class on time, the bump was accidental, and the guy said, "Excuse me," but you think because the guy was bigger he was being a bully.

- You have a problem, and you say that no one will help you. What's really happening: You have not shared your problem with anyone and don't intend to because you think other people are always selfish.

- Someone left a CD player and headphones on the library table. You think that you should take them for yourself because if you don't, someone else will.

Write another example and explain.

_____

_____

_____

4. Blaming Others

Blaming Others means that you do not take responsibility for your own behavior. Instead, you blame other people for your harmful behavior when it is really your fault. It can also mean that you think that your bad behaviors are OK because you were high on drugs or in a bad mood, or because you were once the victim of discrimination or abuse.

Examples

- "I got mixed up with the wrong people." What really happened: You agreed to help your friend take something that belonged to someone else.

- "I was drunk when I beat up that new guy." What really happened: You and your friends were drinking and thought it would be fun to beat up the new guy. You knew it was wrong!
- "She got me mad and got me thinking about those times I was abused. That got me even madder, and I had to lash out." What really happened: The young woman told you to leave her alone, that she didn't want to talk with you. You became angry and punched her in the face. You didn't punch the young man, who is bigger and stronger than you are, when he told you the same thing.

Write another example and explain.

_____

_____

_____

Are thinking and behaving connected? Explain.

_____

_____

_____

How many thinking errors do you have? _____

What are your most common thinking errors?

Number 1 thinking error _____

Number 2 thinking error _____

Number 3 thinking error _____

By identifying your thinking errors you have taken a big step in helping yourself to correct faulty thinking. It takes a strong person to admit to thinking errors and the behavioral problems they cause.

Problems and Thinking Errors Daily Log

Name _____ Date _____

When did this happen? Morning ☐ Afternoon ☐ Evening ☐

Where were you?

Class ☐ Living unit ☐ Dining room ☐ Hallway ☐ Group meeting ☐ Other_____

What kind of behavior/social problem(s) did you have?

☐ Low Self-Image   ☐ Misleads Others
☐ Inconsiderate of Self   ☐ Easily Misled
☐ Inconsiderate of Others   ☐ Alcohol or Drug Problem
☐ Authority Problem   ☐ Stealing
☐ Easily Angered   ☐ Lying
☐ Aggravates Others   ☐ Fronting

What was your thinking error?

☐ Self-Centered   ☐ Minimizing/Mislabeling
☐ Blaming Others (includes blaming bad mood)   ☐ Assuming the Worst

Describe the situation in which you showed your problem(s).

_____

_____

_____

What were you thinking during and after the problem situation? (Describe the thinking error.)

_____

_____

I reported this problem and thinking error in a mutual help meeting on _____ *(date)*.

☐ I did get the meeting.   ☐ I did not get the meeting.

In response to the problem(s), my action plan is as follows:

_____

_____

_____

A plan must be written and fulfilled even if you did not receive the meeting.

How angry were you?
Do not complete this section until your coach or equipper tells you to do so.

☐ 1–burning mad   ☐ 2–really mad   ☐ 3–moderately angry   ☐ 4–mildly angry   ☐ 5–not angry at all

How did you handle yourself?

☐ 1–poorly   ☐ 2–not so well   ☐ 3–OK   ☐ 4–Well   ☐ 5–Great

I won't have this/these problem(s) in the future if I . . .

_____

_____

Keep this log until your coach tells you it may be thrown away.

Ground Rules

Name _____ Date _____

1. Group meetings are sacred!
Write your ideas of why group meetings would be considered so important as to be called sacred.

_____

_____

_____

2. Group meetings begin and end on time.
Is it important to do things when you are supposed to do them? Why?

_____

_____

Will the group be allowed to leave the meeting early or stay beyond the end of the group meeting? Explain.

_____

_____

_____

3. Bring to group only those items needed for the meeting.
How would you feel if someone was playing with something or writing while you were sharing your thoughts, feelings, and behaviors?

_____

_____

_____

4. Each person must participate.
Why is it important for all group members to talk in the meetings?

_____

_____

_____

5. Only one person talks at a time.
If by mistake you interrupt someone, what should you say to that person?

_____

_____

_____

6. Listen to the person who is talking.
Is waiting your turn to talk the same as listening? Explain.

_____

_____

_____

7. If you disagree with someone, do so respectfully.
Why?

_____

_____

_____

8. If you criticize someone, give the person a chance to respond.
How do you feel when you are criticized?

_____

_____

_____

Why is it important to give the person a chance to respond?

_____

_____

_____

9. Never put down or threaten anyone.
Label the problems and possible thinking errors represented by put-downs and threats. Explain.

_____

_____

_____

10. Stay on the subject.
Why is it important to stay on the subject?

_____

_____

_____

11. Keep profanity to a minimum.
What problem label should you suggest that a group member substitute for "pissed-off"? If someone is applying for a job should he or she use profanity? Why not?

_____

_____

_____

12. All issues discussed are confidential.
Explain what this means.

_____

_____

_____

13. Leave the meeting room in as good or better condition than you found it.
Why?

_____

_____

_____

_____

Parts of the Mutual Help Meeting

Name _____ Date _____

Introduction

Your coach talks during this time. Your group listens.

Your coach begins the meeting with thoughts about the previous meetings, suggestions for how to improve your meeting, reminders about the use of the skills and techniques you discussed in equipment meetings, evaluation of the group's progress, encouraging comments, and maybe even challenges. The coach may read the staff team's progress report about you or another group member. This takes approximately 5 minutes.

Problem and thinking error reporting

You and your group members talk to one another. Your coach watches and asks questions or makes brief comments to get your group to think and talk about things.

You and your peers report the problems and thinking errors they have had since the last meeting or raise another problem not yet brought to the attention of the group. The problems are described by using the twelve problem names and the four thinking error labels. It is important that you describe the situation in which your problem and the underlying thinking error happened. Sometimes you or your group members may want to identify all of the problems that occurred in one situation. For instance, a participant who blew up at another group member in the cafeteria and started to fight, even though the teacher instructed the participant to sit down and be quiet, may be awarded the meeting for Easily Angered and whatever his or her thinking error was at the time. The group should not pile on a bunch of other problems (Authority Problem, Inconsiderate of Self, Inconsiderate of Others, and so on) or other thinking errors. The original social/behavioral problem and thinking error should be the focus. You may point out that initial problems caused other problems, but the goal is to remain focused on the original problem and thinking error.

Problem reporting is not a time to discuss or complain about the school or some other situation that you or your group has no control over. The problems to be reported are yours or your group member's own thinking errors and related behavioral problems.

If you would like to have the meeting, you can ask for it at this time, or you can wait until the "awarding the meeting" discussion. You may also request the meeting to tell your life story or have your release meeting.

Problem reporting takes no more than 15 minutes in an experienced group. Each day you are to use the Problems and Thinking Errors Daily Log to identify your problems and thinking errors.

Awarding the meeting

Your group talks together to decide who will get the meeting. Your coach continues to listen, makes comments, or asks questions to help the group think and act responsibly.

Following problem reporting, your group will decide who needs the meeting the most and will also make the best use of the meeting. Everyone in your group is to agree that the person should be awarded the meeting; this is called "reaching a consensus." You simply state who you think should get the meeting. You may or may not offer a short explanation of why you think so. You may change your mind if the group is struggling to make a decision and if you think it would be reasonable to change your mind. Simply state that you have changed your mind—you may or may not offer a reason for it. When awarding the meeting it is important to be as flexible as possible without hurting yourself or anyone else. This part of your meeting takes about 10 minutes. Remember, sometimes it is best to give up the meeting yourself to help one of your group members.

Problem and thinking error analysis and resolution

As before, your group talks, and the coach watches and guides with questions or comments. During this part of the meeting it is especially important to use the information discussed in the equipment meetings. Your coach may remind you to do this.

The group member who was awarded the meeting starts this part of the meeting. He or she repeats the problem(s) and thinking error(s) and describes the situation in which they occurred. You and other group members listen and offer your observations, thoughts, and reactions to the group member. You may ask questions about the person's past behavior and relationships to see how they may or may not be like the current problem(s). This "analysis" of the problem(s) and thinking error(s) may lead your group and the individual to a more accurate renaming and understanding of the problem(s) and thinking error(s). It is important for your group to take its time during the discussion.

Your group's attention and efforts are then directed toward resolution of the problem. The resolution is an action plan that the person awarded the meeting can and will complete. If needed, you and other group members may volunteer or be required to assist in carrying out the plan. This part of the meeting takes 30 to 40 minutes.

Summary

Your coach talks; the group listens.

Your coach summarizes what the group did during the meeting, praises positive group and individual efforts, challenges for better performance, and may remind you of things you learned in the equipment meetings and now need to review. The coach may suggest other ways of improving your meetings, remind you of problems that were reported and still need attention because that person did not get the meeting, and make brief announcements about events outside the meeting. An announcement might be, for example, "Because the buses will be delayed half an hour because of a weather problem, you will have to wait in the cafeteria."

Your Turn: Parts of the Mutual Help Meeting

Name _____ Date _____

Briefly explain the different parts of a mutual help meeting.

Introduction

_____

_____

_____

_____

_____

Problem and thinking error reporting

_____

_____

_____

_____

_____

Awarding the meeting

_____

_____

_____

_____

_____

Problem and thinking error analysis and resolution

_____

_____

_____

_____

_____

Summary

_____

_____

_____

_____

_____

Life Story Meeting

Name _____ Date _____

Your life story helps the group to see how you view yourself and others, and what behavior problems and thinking errors are likely to occur while in the program. By telling your life story, you are improving the group's closeness based on personal sharing, thus creating an investment in your group and in each individual with whom you are sharing. Shortly after entering the program, you are required to write your life story. You are also required to request a group meeting to tell your life story. Before you tell your life story, most or all of the other group members will share their life stories with you. Participants who have been in the group longer will tell you their life stories outside the meeting at a time convenient to both of you. It is important to listen very respectfully while they tell their stories. It takes a strong person to do this.

The group will mostly listen while you tell your life story, but it is expected that they will ask you questions to increase their understanding of your relationships and problems. Examples of appropriate questions are "What were you thinking about when you did that?" and "Were there other times when you did things like that?"

It is important that group members avoid asking "Why" questions—for example, "Why did you do that?" These questions will slow down the storytelling: You or another group member may not know why or may want to avoid talking about a controversial issue. "How are you going to deal with that?" is another question that should be avoided while someone is telling a life story. The telling of the life story is each person's opportunity to share information and increase the sense of belonging within the group.

When you have completed your life story, your group then assigns you the social/behavioral and thinking errors they think you should resolve or be in the process of resolving by the time you leave the program.

1. When are you required to write your life story?

   _____

   _____

2. When do participants who have been in the group longer tell you their life stories?

   _____

   _____

3. What are the purposes in telling your life story?

   _____

   _____

4. What should the group do while you tell your life story?

   _____

   _____

5. Write an example of an appropriate and an inappropriate question to ask during a life story.

   _____

   _____

6. What does the group do when you complete your life story?

   _____

   _____

My Life Story

Name _____ Age _____ Birthday _____

Place of birth _____ Ethnic group _____

Family information

_____

_____

Where and with whom I have lived (most recent first)

_____

_____

_____

_____

_____

Things that have happened in my life (include when they happened)

_____

_____

_____

_____

_____

Important things that the group and staff should know about me (include special skills and talents)

_____

_____

_____

_____

My most common problems and thinking errors

_____

_____

My short-term plans

_____

_____

My long-range plans

_____

_____

_____

Release/Discharge Meeting Questions

Name _____ Date _____

Answer these questions as honestly and completely as you can.

1. List your behavior/social problems and thinking errors.

    a. Assigned to you by the group when you told your life story

    _____

    _____

    _____

    b. Identified later by you and/or the group

    _____

    _____

    _____

2. How have your thinking errors and problems affected you and other people?

_____

_____

_____

3. List the three other people affected the most. Explain how.

_____

_____

_____

4. How have your thinking and behavior changed? Include specific examples of the things you have done to correct the harm you have caused.

_____

_____

_____

5. Which group members have you helped with problems and how? Provide specific examples.

_____

_____

_____

6. What are your short- and long-term plans for the future (school, job, support groups, etc.)?

_____

_____

_____

7. What do you think your group will say about your request for a recommendation for release?

_____

_____

_____

Coach's Mutual Help Meeting Overview

Date/time _____ Coach _____ Group _____ Location/room no. _____

This form is for notations before, during, and after the meeting.

Pre-meeting notes

Issues to be mentioned during the introduction, progress reports to be read, issues from previous meeting to watch for, individuals to be encouraged, etc.

_____

_____

Problem and thinking error reporting and seating

List the names in the order of seating.

Name	Problem(s)	Thinking error(s)	Situation
1.			
2.			
3.			
4.			
5.			
6.			
7.			
8.			
9.			

Problem and thinking error reporting

What happened during problem reporting, process issues to be corrected, interventions made, positive or negative interpersonal interactions, accuracy of problem and thinking error reporting, length of reporting, etc.

_____

_____

_____

Awarding the meeting

Who was awarded the meeting? _____ Specific problem(s) _____ Thinking error(s) _____

Situation _____

Notes *(time, process issues, interventions, follow-up needed, etc.)* _____

_____

Problem and thinking error analysis and resolution

Degree of problem reidentification needed, group attentiveness, related historical problem(s), cognitive skills used, interventions and effect, notes on individuals, action plan, staff to be notified, follow-up needed, etc.

_____

_____

_____

Summary notes

Notes are to be made before or during the meeting for use in the summary: comments for individuals and group, announcements, social skills use, handouts for the next equipment meeting, etc.

_____

_____

_____

Post-meeting notes

Developmental stage of the group, interpersonal interaction issues, amount and type of intervention used/needed, staff/youth follow-up, issues for future meetings, needs of individuals, need for carefully observing teller of life story, requirement for asking other staff to reinforce individuals and/or group, etc.

_____

_____

_____

Coach's Mutual Help Meeting Overview • page 2 of 2

Observer's Report and Critique of Mutual Help Meetings

This form is used to assist the coach in becoming a better group leader. Before the meeting, make four to six copies of page 4 of this form ("Problem and Thinking Error Analysis and Resolution").

Date/time _____ Group _____

Coach _____ Observer _____

Coach's overall preparation

Review of progress reports, school meetings and responses, parent participation, etc.

_____

_____

Stage of group development (*circle one*): forming storming norming positive peer culture

Introduction plan

Equipment meeting concepts or skills to be mentioned, reports to be shared, appropriate use of the meeting format and times, etc.

_____

_____

Was the coach prepared to begin the meeting? (*Written notes, follow-up items from last meeting, etc.*)

_____

☐ yes ☐ no Was the room vacant and ready for the group meeting?

☐ yes ☐ no Was the coach on time for the meeting?

☐ yes ☐ no Was the coach appropriately positive, attentive, and energetic upon the group's arrival?

Group's behavior and demeanor upon entry

Consider verbal and nonverbal behaviors in evaluating demeanor.

☐ On time   ☐ Positive—ready for the meeting, smiles!

☐ Tardy   ☐ Indifferent—scheduled to be there.

                ☐ Negative—resistant, sullen, don't want to there.

Comments _____

_____

Introduction

What did the coach say? Was the introduction plan fulfilled?

Beginning time _____

Problem and thinking error reporting and seating

List the names in the order of seating.

Beginning time _____

Name	Problem(s)	Thinking error(s)	Situation
1.			
2.			
3.			
4.			
5.			
6.			
7.			
8.			
9.			

Problem and thinking error reporting interventions

Note times and describe the coach's interventions and the resulting discussion among/effect on group members. The first item is given as an example.

Time	Coach's intervention	Discussion/effect on group
3:22	Can the group identify another problem that Sam has shown?	Matt stated that Sam had an Authority Problem in math class. Sam agreed and shared his thinking error and the situation.

Awarding the meeting

Beginning time _____

Who was awarded the meeting? _____ Situation _____

Specific problem(s) _____ Thinking error(s) _____

Was the meeting awarded to someone who: ☐ yes ☐ no Needed it? ☐ yes ☐ no Wanted it? ☐ yes ☐ no Would use it?

Comments _____

Problem and thinking error analysis and resolution
Use your copies of page 4 of this form to note times and describe the coach's interventions and resulting discussion/effect on group members.

Summary
Record the coach's general comments and specific feedback to participants, any specific techniques used (e.g., "punch and burp"), and other pertinent comments.

Beginning time _____

_____

_____

Meeting ending time _____

Did the group leave the room in as good or better shape than they found it? ☐ yes ☐ no

Group's demeanor at the end of the meeting ☐ positive ☐ indifferent ☐ negative

Comments and suggestions
Review the entire observation form before filling in this section. Be sure to identify the coach's strengths and the areas where improvement is needed. Suggest ways of improving, and offer examples.

_____

_____

_____

_____

_____

Problem and thinking error analysis and resolution

Note times and describe the coach's interventions and the resulting discussion among/effect on group members.

Beginning time _____

Time	Coach's intervention	Discussion/effect on group

SECTION FOUR

Equipment Meetings

INTRODUCTION

Although the mutual help meetings described in Section 3 promote the necessary positive youth culture, positively motivated youths still need "equipment" (anger management/thinking error correction skills, social skills, and social decision making skills) to be effective in helping one another. Unequipped youth, however well intentioned, eventually experience frustration; once frustrated, they often fall back on put-downs and threats, and fail to promote responsible thinking and acting in others and themselves. Research has shown the critical importance of adding—as the EQUIP program does through "equipment meetings"—cognitive interventions to behavioral programs. In the EQUIP program, cognitive treatment provides helping skills that reduce frustration and destructive group behavior; the youths can thereby become more effective agents of change for one another.

Specific materials to help you implement these meetings are provided in Sections 5, 6, and 7 of this guide. To help you get an overview of the content of the equipment meetings, the table beginning on the next page gives the curriculum "in a nutshell." As shown, the curricular components are presented as "rounds" in a recommended sequence. For example, the first round of equipment meetings includes Evaluating Anger/Aggression (anger management/correcting thinking errors), Expressing a Complaint Constructively (social skills training), and the Martian's Adviser's Problem Situation (social decision making). Sequencing meetings in this way heightens interest, permits learning across the curriculum, and promotes emergence of the themes of helping others and becoming less self-centered as the group progresses through the program.

A final equipment meeting, entitled "Up or Down," is intended as a review and consolidation of participants' learning during the entire equipment meeting cycle.

The Equipment Meeting Curriculum in a Nutshell

Numbers at the top of each box indicate the order in which the different types of meetings are delivered.

Anger Management/ Thinking Error Correction	Social Skills	Social Decision Making
1 **Evaluating and relabeling anger/aggression** Reevaluating, relabeling Anger management, not elimination	**2** **Expressing a Complaint Constructively** Think ahead what you'll say, etc. Say how you contributed to the problem. Make a constructive suggestion.	**3** **Martian's Adviser's Problem** Planet A is seen as self-centered Planet B labeled truly strong Making the group Planet B
4 **Anatomy of anger (AMBC)** Mind as the source of anger Early warning signs (body) Anger-reducing self-talk	**5** **Caring for Someone Who Is Sad or Upset** Notice and think ahead. Listen don't interrupt. "Be there."	**6** **Jerry's Problem Situation** Loyalty, commitment Value of close friendships **Mark's Problem Situation** Breaking up in a considerate way Getting even is immature
7 **Monitoring and correcting thinking errors** Gary's Thinking Errors exercise Daily logs	**8** **Dealing Constructively with Negative Peer Pressure** Think, "Why?" Think ahead to consequences. Suggest something else (less harmful).	**9** **Jim's Problem Situation** Can't trust "friend" with a stealing problem Stealing is wrong even from a stranger
10 **More anger reducers** Deep breathing, backward counting, peaceful imagery Anger reducers to "buy time"	**11** **Keeping Out of Fights** Stop and think. Think ahead to consequences. Handle the situation another way.	**12** **Alonzo's Problem Situation** **Sarah's Problem Situation** Shouldn't let friends steal (car, store items) Harm from stealing True friend would not put you on the spot Closing gap between judgment and behavior (relabeling, using social skills)
13 **Thinking ahead to consequences** Thinking ahead (if-then thinking) Types of consequences (especially for others) TOP (think of the other person)	**14** **Helping Others** Think, "Is there a need?" Think ahead how to help, when, etc. Offer to help.	**15** **George's Problem Situation** **Leon's Problem Situation** Should tell on drug-dealing brother, friend planning an escape Others could get killed Important to jail drug dealers

16 **Using "I" statements for constructive consequences** "You" statements (put-downs, threats) Use of "I" statements instead of "you" statements	17 **Preparing for a Stressful Conversation** Imagine ahead your feelings and the other person's feelings (TOP). Think ahead what to say. Think ahead how the other person might reply.	18 **Dave's Problem Situation** Shouldn't deliver drugs for friends Sister's life may be at stake Closing gap between judgment and behavior (relabeling, correcting thinking errors, exhorting)
19 **Self-evaluation** Self-evaluation, self-reflection Talking back to thinking errors Staying constructive	20 **Dealing Constructively with Someone Angry at You** Listen openly and patiently. Think of something you can agree with, say the person is right about that. Apologize or explain, make a constructive suggestion.	21 **Juan's Problem Situation** Should tell on suicidal friend Suicide is Self-Centered thinking error Existential/spiritual concerns
22 **Reversing** Things you do that make other people angry Reversing exercise (correcting Blaming Others error)	23 **Expressing Care and Appreciation** Think if the person would like you to care. Think ahead to what you will say, when, etc. Tell the person how you feel.	24 **Sam's Problem Situation** Should tell on a friend who shoplifted Important to prosecute shoplifters Store owner is not to blame (Blaming Others)
25 **More consequences for others/ correcting distorted self-views** Victims and Victimizers exercise Consequences for victims One's own victimization is no excuse for victimizing others Think of the pain your actions have caused others (TOP)	26 **Dealing Constructively with Someone Accusing You of Something** Think how you feel, tell yourself to calm down. Think if the accuser is right (TOP). If the accuser is right, apologize/make restitution; if wrong, say it isn't true, it's a wrong impression, etc.	27 **Reggie's Problem Situation** Should reveal violent dad's drinking Should do what's best for the family Wouldn't want someone to lie to you But mother is wrong to put Reggie on the spot
28 **Victimizer and grand review** Mind of the Victimizer exercise Conclusion of consciousness raising	29 **Responding Constructively to Failure** Ask if you did fail. Think what you could do differently. Decide, plan to try again.	30 **Antonio's Problem Situation** Shouldn't help friend cheat Can't trust "friend" with cheating problem Correcting thinking errors

31 **The Final Session: Up or Down?**

(33 thoughts, skills, behaviors)
Up represents mature, accurate, constructive, responsible.
Down represents immature, inaccurate, distorted, destructive, irresponsible.
    Spans all three curriculum components and provides opportunites for motivational comments.
    Tests knowledge of the content of curriculum components.
    Encourages the use of concepts or skills learned in equipment meetings to help others and self.

SECTION FIVE

Anger Management/ Thinking Error Correction

INTRODUCTION

Anger and aggression are, of course, common among antisocial youth. It is not surprising that the most frequently reported problem in the mutual help meeting is Easily Angered. Antisocial behavior that is aggressive is not only "thoughtless" or deficient but also involves cognitive distortions or "errors of thinking." The materials provided in this section are designed to help correct these thinking errors. Youths can also learn to recognize and begin to correct these thinking errors by playing *EQUIPPED for Life* (Horn, Shively, & Gibbs, 2001), a highly valuable new therapeutic board game, available from Research Press.

It is important to note that these meetings offer an opportunity for participants to view anger and aggression from a distance: The youths' personal examples may be used but are not to be discussed in depth—save that for the mutual help meetings. Keep the anger management meetings a "step back" from personal experience to allow for objectivity.

As the meeting proceeds, listen for thinking errors and point them out, using "ask, don't tell" or other constructive interventions whenever possible (see pp. 23–32 of the EQUIP book). Reinforce positive remarks. Let the group do most of the work!

FORMAT OF THE ANGER MANAGEMENT/ THINKING ERROR CORRECTION MEETING

The instructional plan for anger management/thinking error correction meetings includes an overview of activities, list of materials, and step-by-step procedural instructions for conducting the meeting (i.e., Equipper's Guidelines). Each meeting after the first one begins with a review of the previous session, followed by the instructional sequence. Meetings end with a wrap-up summary of the content covered and identification of the topic for the next session.

ACTIVITIES AND MATERIALS

To prepare for anger management meetings, equippers should do as follows:

1. Read chapter 4 in the EQUIP book, giving particular attention to the "Procedure and Leader Notes" section for each meeting. Also review pages 143–147 in EQUIP for discussion of TOP ("think of the other person").

2. An easel pad is necessary for many of the sessions. Before each pertinent session, check that there is paper for the pad, two markers (preferably different colors, to distinguish ideas), and masking tape to hang the completed sheets on the wall. If possible, leave the pages there, as they will be a useful reference and reminder in other equipment meetings, as well as in mutual help meetings.

3. Before each meeting, photocopy enough Participant Handouts so every group member may have one.

4. After each meeting, fill out the Equipper's Review and Self-Evaluation Form for anger management/thinking error correction.

The Equipper's Guidelines for each of the anger management/thinking error correction meetings, mentioned earlier, are new to this guide, as are the various Participant Handouts.

Session 1: Evaluating and Relabeling Anger and Aggression

Overview of activities

- Discussion of anger and aggression, benefits of controlling anger

- Relabeling of anger and aggression (as weak, immature, counterproductive, etc.) and nonviolence (as putting youths in a stronger position by giving them options besides fighting)

- Expression of a qualifier, important for "selling" the program: The goal of these equipment meetings is anger management, not to eliminate anger or to convince anyone that fighting is always wrong.

Materials

- Participant Handout: Evaluating and Relabeling Anger and Aggression

Procedure

1. Discuss and record the advantages and disadvantages of anger and aggression.

> Advantages
> > Self-defense
> >
> > Feeling powerful
> >
> > Getting even
>
> Disadvantages
> > Causes more problems
> >
> > Feeling embarrassed/stupid
> >
> > Losing friends
> >
> > Losing people's trust

2. Present and discuss the ideas in the following example.

> - Anger is something everyone experiences.
> - Strong people control their anger (relabel self-control as powerful by using the self-control of athletes as an illustration).
> - Weak people do not have self-control. They become violent.

3. To emphasize this last point, relabel uncontrolled anger as weak and foolish by using the example of the Clown—or Clowns?—in the Ring.*

The clown in the ring is the guy who's trying to start a fight. *(Indicate drawing A.)* He's a clown and a fool because he's not thinking of all the disadvantages of anger and violence. His goal is to make you a fool, too, to draw you into the circus ring with him. He wants to attach his strings to you. *(Draw strings as in B.)* Then he can pull on the strings and draw you into the ring with him. If you let him attach the strings and pull you in, then who's in control? And he wins if you start fighting. How many clowns are there in the ring now? *(Indicate C.)*

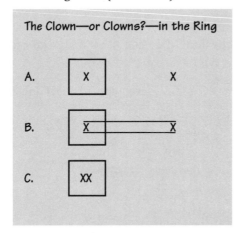

4. Suggest that anger is OK if it is used to motivate constructive behavior (e.g., self-defense; assertive, not aggressive, behavior). Listen for thinking errors and point them out using "ask, don't tell" or other constructive interventions when possible.

5. Finally, discuss the benefits of managing anger.

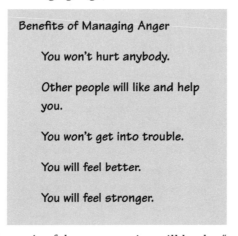

6. Let participants know that the topic of the next meeting will be the "anatomy" of anger.

Session 1: Evaluating and Relabeling Anger and Aggression

Name _____ Date _____

Everyone feels anger, but not everyone manages (controls) anger well. Anger can be an advantage if it is properly managed or a disadvantage if it is not properly managed.

1. Is feeling angry wrong or bad?   ☐ yes ☐ no

    Why or why not?

    _____

2. List some advantages of anger.

    _____

3. List some disadvantages of anger.

    _____

4. List some situations in which you have become angry.

    _____

5. Draw the Clown—or Clowns?—in the Ring, and explain what this diagram means.

6. Has someone who was acting like a clown ever pulled you into the ring?   ☐ yes ☐ no

    What kind of "strings" did you let that person attach to you to pull you into the ring? For example: name calling, challenging you in front of others, making remarks about your family.

    _____

    _____

7. Have you ever been the clown trying to pull someone into the ring with you?   ☐ yes ☐ no

    What strings did you use to try to make that person into a clown like you?

    _____

8. List four benefits of managing your anger.

    _____

    _____

Session 2: Anatomy of Anger (AMBC)

Overview of activities

- Review of Session 1

- Introduction to the anatomy of anger (AMBC)

- Instruction in the basic thesis of the program: It is your mind (attitude, belief, what you tell yourself) that makes you angry, not the event "out there"

- Attention to the early warning signs of anger (B)

- Self-talk reducers (M) that help a person buy time

Materials

- Participant Handouts

  Self-Talk Anger Reducers

  Anatomy of Anger (AMBC)

Procedure

1. Use the Equipper's Guidelines from the previous session to review. Explain that the present session will help the group learn about the "anatomy" of anger.

2. Inform the group that the acronym that will help them remember the process is AMBC. Start with A, then do B, C, and M.

   A: The *activating event* is the thing that leads to your anger. These events are also called "hot spots." What are some of your hot spots?

   B: What do you usually feel or see happening right after the hot spot? What do you think B stands for? *(Body reaction)* Reactions in your body are early warning signs of anger.

   C: What do you think C stands for? *(You may have to provide "Consequences.")*

   M: What do you think M stands for? *(Mind activity)* Is your body reacting to the hot spot or to what is going on in your mind? *(Participants respond.)* That's right, your body is reacting to your mind. It is reacting to the "self-talk" going on in your mind.

3. Valuable points of discussion:

   One is not always aware of one's mind activity.

   Mind activity or an angry attitude can very quickly cause a body reaction.

   It is very important to become aware of our thoughts so we can do something about them.

A = Activating Event
   Getting hit, put-downs, threats, being dissed, someone stealing my stuff, getting picked on by a bully

M = Mind Activity
   I'm getting my respect back.
   I'm not taking this anymore.
   I'll teach him/hurt them.

B = Body Reaction
   Fast breathing, getting hot
   Tense neck, shoulders, fists
   Sweaty hands
   Clenched teeth

C = Consequences
   Fighting
   Write-ups
   Arguing and threats
   Being kicked out of school
   Making enemies

4. Tell participants to be aware of the early warning signs and use them as signals to do something about the thoughts that are causing them. Say, "When you feel the warning signs, you are not in control. The other person is in control because you are buying into him or her."

5. Remind group members of the Clown—or Clowns?—in the Ring concept, presented in Session 1. Tell them, "If you want to be in control, you've got to change your mind activity from thoughts that make you lose control to thoughts that put you into self-control."

6. Ask, "What are some calming thoughts you could use as self-talk to reduce your anger?" These are called self-talk anger reducers. Distribute copies of the Self-Talk Anger Reducers handout and have participants refer to it as needed.

7. Conclude by saying, "Mind activity causing anger usually involves thinking errors. So self-talk anger reducers must include corrections of those thinking errors. In our next anger management meeting we will discuss correcting thinking errors.

Session 2: Self-Talk Anger Reducers

Name _____ Date _____

Keep this list.

Before an activating event

"This could be a bad situation, but I believe in myself."

"Try not to take this too seriously."

Positive mind activity during an activating event

"I'm going to keep my cool and let this guy get in trouble."

"If he wants to make a fool of himself he can, but he's not gonna make a fool out of me."

"Time for a few deep breaths."

"It's really a shame he has to act like that."

"He's the one with the problem."

"He can be OK when he's not showing his Aggravates Others problem."

"I don't even have to look at him. I'll just walk away and not let it get to me. I don't need to prove myself."

"Maybe I took it the wrong way."

"I'm not going to get pushed around, but I'm not going haywire either."

"He'd probably like me to get really angry. Well, I'm going to disappoint him."

"I can't expect people to act the way I want them to."

"Think ahead—don't lose your head."

After an activating event

When the conflict is unresolved

"These are tough situations, and they take time to straighten out."

"I'll get better at this as I get more practice."

"It could have been a lot worse."

When the conflict is resolved or coping has been successful

"I handled that one pretty well. That wasn't as hard as I thought. It worked!"

"I actually got through that without getting angry. I'm doing better at this all the time."

"I thought ahead. It worked."

Session 2: Anatomy of Anger (AMBC)

Name _____ Date _____

Our thoughts have a lot to do with what we become angry about and how we manage our anger. Sometimes our thoughts happen so quickly that we don't even know they happened. This is especially true when the experience is something that has happened many times.

Anger is made up of four parts. We use the letters **AMBC** to help us remember the parts.

1. **A** stands for _____ .

   These events are also called "hot spots." List some of your hot spots.

   _____

   _____

   Do **B** then **C**, then come back and do **M**.

2. **M** stands for _____ .

3. **B** stands for _____ .

   List some of the things that happen to your body when you get angry.

   _____

   _____

   When you feel these early warning signs are you at risk for losing control? ___ yes ___ no

4. **C** stands for _____ .

   List some examples of things that happen when you let your anger get out of control.

   _____

   _____

5. *(Fill in the blanks.)* The **M** goes between the **A** and the **B** because your **B** _____ is reacting to your **M** _____, NOT the **A** _____.

6. Give one example of a self-talk anger reducer you can use in the following situations.

   Before an activating event

   _____

   During an activating event

   _____

   For an unresolved conflict

   _____

   _____

   For a resolved conflict

   _____

   _____

Session 3: Monitoring and Correcting Thinking Errors

Overview of activities

- Review of Session 2
- Learning and correcting the thinking errors
- Monitoring the thinking errors in everyday behavior (introducing the Self-Help Daily Logs)

Materials

- Participant Handouts

  Gary's Thinking Errors

  Problems and Thinking Errors Daily Log

  Positive Behaviors Daily Log

Procedure

1. Use the Equipper's Guidelines from the previous session to present a thorough review. Tell the group that the present session will focus on the mind, especially thinking errors.

2. Repeat the idea that the meaning attached to the activating event by the mind, not the activating event itself, causes anger. Explain that special attention must be given to the thoughts (and possibly thinking errors) that quickly follow the activating event.

3. Use the example of standing in line to underscore the idea that anger-arousing mind activity often involves thinking errors. Ask, "Who has felt angry when standing in a long line? *(Participants respond.)* You may have thought, 'This is unfair—I shouldn't have to wait in this line' But that's a thinking error. Why?" *(Others have to wait, too. I'm no exception.)* Prompt the group to identify Self-Centered as the thinking error.

4. Distribute copies of Gary's Thinking Errors. Have the group read the scenario silently. Write the abbreviations for the thinking errors along the left-hand column of the easel pad (SC = Self-Centered; MM = Minimizing/Mislabeling; AW = Assuming the Worst; BO = Blaming Others). Leave a space about 8 inches at the bottom of the page.

5. Next, ask the questions listed on the handout. (See the following chart for an example of what the entire easel pad might look like after all of the questions have been answered.)

   - *Question 1: What thoughts ran through Gary's head, do you think, both during the situation and afterward?* Have a participant read this question aloud. Write the group's ideas of Gary's thoughts under the abbreviations for the most applicable thinking errors. (Answers may be moved later, if needed.)

   - *Question 2: What are the errors in these thoughts? Cecilia was mad at Gary because he did something to hurt her. What do you think that might have been?* Ask another participant to read the first part of this question: Tell participants that the abbreviations at the left of the easel pad are hints to the answers (i.e., Self-Centered, Minimizing/Mislabeling, Assuming the Worst, Blaming Others). Have yet another volunteer read the second part of Question 2 aloud; record the group's answers.

   - *Question 3: How might Gary have "'talked back" to his thinking errors?* Encourage a group member to read the third question aloud; record positive self-talk examples in the right-hand column of the easel pad, beside the previously written examples of thinking errors.

- *Question 4: If Gary had corrected his thinking errors, would he still have stabbed Cecilia?* This question concludes the Gary's Thinking Errors exercise: The correct response is "NO!" Reinforce that response.

6. Immediately distribute and explain each of the Daily Logs. Tell participants that these are tools they will use to help them monitor and correct their thinking errors.

- *Problems and Thinking Errors:* Tell participants that this log will help them recognize their hot spots and understand just how hot those hot spots are. Explain that this awareness will help them to "check themselves" so they can improve their use of anger reducers and develop replacement thoughts. In other words, it will help them to anticipate and manage their low- and high-risk situations. (This log is basically the same as that used to help with problem reporting in mutual help meetings.)

- *Positive Behaviors:* Explain that participants may also use this log to help them keep track of how often they are following rules and using the information they are learning in the program.

7. Conclude by saying, "Sometimes anger occurs so quickly that you are in trouble before you know it. We will cover techniques to manage that situation in our next anger management meeting."

8. Designate a place where participants can pick up blank logs and let them know where that place is. Inform them that the next meeting will begin with a brief review of the logs.

What Gary thought	What Gary should have thought
SC	
I'm the boss!	I'm no better than she is.
How dare she touch me!	I'd be mad, too.
Who does she think she is?	She deserves better.
MM	
I'll teach her!	You don't teach anybody by stabbing them.
I have to defend myself!	I won't die from a push in the shoulder.
AW	
She hates me.	She's mad now, but she won't stay that way if I sincerely apologize and change.
BO	
She was asking for it.	I started it by treating her badly.
She's the one who left out the knife.	I shouldn't have picked up the knife. It's my fault.

What Gary might have done to hurt Cecilia
He spent the rent money!
He was cheating on her.
He beat her.
He busted up the furniture.

Session 3: Gary's Thinking Errors

Name _____ Date _____

Gary is in the kitchen of his apartment. Gary's girlfriend, Cecilia, is angry at him for something he did to hurt her. She yells at him. She pushes his shoulder. Thoughts run through Gary's head. Gary does nothing to correct the errors in his thoughts. Gary becomes furious. He swears at Cecilia. A sharp kitchen knife is nearby. Gary picks up the knife and stabs Cecilia, seriously wounding her.

1. What thoughts ran through Gary's head, do you think, both during the situation and afterward? Suggest some sample thoughts.

   _____

   _____

   _____

   _____

2. What are the errors in these thoughts? Cecilia was mad at Gary because he did something to hurt her. What do you think that might have been?

   _____

   _____

   _____

   _____

3. What might Gary have told himself in this situation? In other words, how might Gary have "talked back" to his thinking errors? Suggest some things Gary could have said to himself to correct each type of thinking error.

   _____

   _____

   _____

   _____

4. If Gary had corrected his thinking errors, would he still have stabbed Cecilia?

   _____

   _____

   _____

   _____

Session 3: Problems and Thinking Errors Daily Log

Name _____ Date _____

When did this happen?   Morning ☐   Afternoon ☐   Evening ☐

Where were you?

Class ☐   Living unit ☐   Dining room ☐   Hallway ☐   Group meeting ☐   Other_____

What kind of behavior/social problem(s) did you have?

☐ Low Self-Image   ☐ Misleads Others
☐ Inconsiderate of Self   ☐ Easily Misled
☐ Inconsiderate of Others   ☐ Alcohol or Drug Problem
☐ Authority Problem   ☐ Stealing
☐ Easily Angered   ☐ Lying
☐ Aggravates Others   ☐ Fronting

What was your thinking error?

☐ Self-Centered   ☐ Minimizing/Mislabeling
☐ Blaming Others (includes blaming bad mood)   ☐ Assuming the Worst

Describe the situation in which you showed your problem(s).

_____

_____

_____

What were you thinking during and after the problem situation? (Describe the thinking error.)

_____

_____

I reported this problem and thinking error in a mutual help meeting on _____ *(date).*
☐ I did get the meeting.   ☐ I did not get the meeting.
In response to the problem(s), my action plan is as follows:

_____

_____

_____

A plan must be written and fulfilled even if you did not receive the meeting.

How angry were you?
Do not complete this section until your coach or equipper tells you to do so.

☐ 1–burning mad   ☐ 2–really mad   ☐ 3–moderately angry   ☐ 4–mildly angry   ☐ 5–not angry at all

How did you handle yourself?

☐ 1–poorly   ☐ 2–not so well   ☐ 3–OK   ☐ 4–well   ☐ 5–great

I won't have this/these problem(s) in the future if I . . .

_____

_____

Keep this log until your coach tells you it may be thrown away.

Session 3: Positive Behaviors Daily Log

Name _____ Date _____

☐ Morning ☐ Afternoon ☐ Evening

☐ I maintained myself (took shower, took care of clothes, brushed teeth, etc.).

☐ I did my assigned chores.

☐ I followed the safety rules.

☐ I went to classes without being reminded.

☐ I worked hard in classes.

☐ I did the assigned work in class.

☐ I accepted constructive feedback.

☐ I stood up for my rights in a positive way.

☐ I participated in programs I attended.

☐ I accepted responsibility for my actions and did not make an excuse.

☐ I talked somebody out of fighting.

☐ I complimented someone for something he or she did.

☐ I showed consideration for another person.

☐ I *(fill in the blank)* _____

What did you do to help yourself today?

_____

_____

_____

_____

_____

_____

_____

What did you do to help someone else today?

_____

_____

_____

_____

_____

_____

_____

Session 4: More Anger Reducers

Overview of activities

- Review of Session 3

- Instruction and practice in deep breathing, counting backward, pleasant imagery

- Reinforcement of the importance of using self-talk anger reducers to buy time

Materials

- Daily logs (completed since the previous session)

Procedure

1. Use the Equipper's Guidelines from the last session to review "talking back" to thinking errors. Ask the group to share, individually, how the use of the daily logs went.

2. Remind participants that you closed the last anger management session by noting that sometimes anger occurs so quickly that you are in trouble before you know it and that the present session will cover some simple, effective techniques to help control anger: deep breathing, counting backward, and calling up peaceful imagery. Tell group members that it is important to remember and practice these skills because they could even save your life someday.

3. Explain *breathing deeply* by role-playing a basketball scenario as you talk:

   Pretend to be a basketball player who was just fouled and is preparing to shoot the free throws.

   Stand at an imaginary free throw line, then breathe in slowly, hold your breath for a bit, then let it out slowly. Repeat.

   Explain that the deep breathing is helping you relax. Breathe one more time, then shoot the ball.

4. Have the group repeat some of their activating events (hot spots), and write these on the easel pad. Tell them to imagine a hot spot is happening and then practice deep breathing while imagining the event.

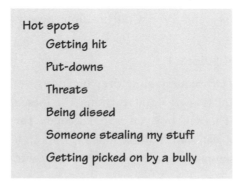

   Hot spots
       Getting hit
       Put-downs
       Threats
       Being dissed
       Someone stealing my stuff
       Getting picked on by a bully

5. Ask, "Could you feel that helping?" Discuss the experience, drawing out participants' reactions and giving positive feedback.

6. Tell group members, "Another neat little trick is to silently and slowly count backward from 20 to 1. Sometimes you can just turn away from the hot spot while you are counting." Explain that you will now ask them to combine counting backward and slow, deep breathing to gain as much self-control power as possible:

Let's try both of these things together. OK, imagine your worst hot spot. *(Allow 10 seconds.)*

Now get the deep breathing started. *(Model; make sure group is breathing deeply.)*

Next we'll count aloud from 20. Now start. *(Model; start counting aloud backward; make sure group members are both breathing deeply and counting.)*

Could you feel that helping? *(Discuss.)* Of course, when you're using this technique you'll be counting silently.

Let's try deep breathing and counting backward silently. *(Lead the group in deep breathing. Remind them that they should be counting backward silently.)*

7. Explain that the third anger-reducing technique is to imagine pleasant or peaceful scenes:

   You can calm yourself down from angry mind activity by imagining a pleasant or peaceful scene. This is a lot like calming self-talk, except that we use mental pictures instead of thoughts. What are some happy or peaceful scenes you can imagine? *(Through discussion, make a list on the easel pad.)*

   > Peaceful scenes
   >   Sunbathing
   >   Walking in the park with
   >   boyfriend or girlfriend
   >   Relaxing on couch

   It's pretty hard to be saying to yourself how you're going to tear somebody's head off while you're imagining yourself sunbathing on the beach!

8. Have the group practice using all three techniques at once:

   First, think of that activating event. *(Allow 8 seconds.)*

   Start slow, deep breathing. *(Model; make sure group members are breathing deeply.)*

   Now start counting backward from 20, silently. *(Allow 8 seconds.)*

   Now imagine your favorite peaceful scene while breathing deeply and counting backward. *(Allow 8 seconds.)*

   Could you feel that helping? *(Discuss.)*

9. Tell the group, "These three techniques—slow, deep breathing; counting backward; and pleasant imagery—will help reduce those angry body reactions. Use these three things together for maximum anger-control power. They will buy you crucial seconds. They would have bought Gary crucial seconds, right? Then you can start to think straight. You can reduce your anger even more with calming self-talk and with self-talk that corrects the errors in your thinking."

10. Encourage group members to try these techniques outside the group, letting them know that they will be asked during the next session how their practice went.

11. Close by describing the focus of the next session: learning two peaceful self-talk techniques for reducing anger. Remind participants to continue using their daily logs.

Session 5: Thinking Ahead to Consequences

Overview of activities

- Review of Session 4
- Learning thinking ahead to consequences (if-then thinking)
- Learning TOP (think of the other person)

Materials

- Daily logs (completed since the previous session)
- Thinking Ahead to Consequences Chart (prepared before the session begins)

Procedure

You are required to provide a lot of the information and energy in this meeting. It is still important to involve participants to the maximum extent possible.

1. Use the Equipper's Guidelines from the previous session to review. Inquire how group members felt about their experiences using the relaxation techniques. Ask the group to share, individually, how their use of the daily logs is going.

2. Introduce the idea of thinking ahead: "Today we're going to get back to self-talk techniques for reducing anger. What self-talk techniques have we learned so far?" Discuss calming self-talk and correcting thinking errors.

3. Explain that the self-talk techniques for today are very powerful ones. The first one is called *thinking ahead to consequences,* or "if-then" thinking: If I do this negative thing, then that negative consequence will follow, so I'd better not do it.

4. Suggest that group members can use thinking ahead even before they're in a hot spot—in fact, to prevent one. For example:

    Let's say you have a car and it's in the repair shop, and you know you've had problems in the past when picking your car up at the repair shop. So now your car is in the shop again, and you can think ahead. You can think: When I go to pick up my car at the repair shop, it may not be ready. So you're thinking ahead to a consequence right there. And your thinking ahead might result in your thinking of something you can do right now, before you even get to the shop. What's that? *(Discuss telephoning ahead to make sure the car is in fact ready.)*

    OK, let's say the people at the repair shop said it would be ready, but you realize that when you get to the shop you may find it still isn't. So you can think ahead: What if this happens? How will I feel? *(Discuss the feelings of frustration and anger.)*

    Still keep thinking ahead. What will be the consequences if you lose control? *(Ask the group to suggest some possible consequences.)*

5. Tell the group to use if-then self-talk to say, "Think ahead! If I give up my self-control and hit the guy, they'll call the police. I might get arrested. Plus, they'll have my car." More self-talk: "I'd better stay calm and remember how to stay out of fights. This is good thinking ahead!"

6. Discuss all the likely consequences of losing control and hitting or even swearing at the other person: "Maybe immediately you would feel better, but it may just provoke the person to fight. Someone may even get hurt, and the problem still wouldn't be solved. Chances are it will not end there."

7. Point out the importance of thinking ahead to all the possible consequences, not just those that may happen early on. State to the group, "You've got to think ahead, both to first-off consequences and to later consequences. So far, we have talked about consequences to yourself, but it's important to consider consequences for the other person."

8. Explain that thinking ahead can be used for situations that do not involve anger, such as skipping school, stealing a car, or even using drugs. (The example of stealing a car is outlined in the EQUIP book, pp. 145–146.)

9. Present a scenario appropriate to the group. For example: "Let's take skipping school. If I skip school, I will probably get caught, my mom will be called, and I will be punished at school and at home. Also, I will probably do poorly in school whether I get caught or not."

10. Display the Thinking Ahead to Consequences chart, then use the "ask, don't tell" intervention technique to elicit participant responses concerning the scenario. Use the chart as a roadmap for the rest of the session. As group members speak, record their responses on a separate easel pad sheet.

   - *Step 1:* Ask the following questions to elicit general consequences for self.

     What do you think would happen if you did this?

     What has happened before when you've broken rules?

     What about long-term consequences? Did you lose the trust and respect of other people or get a reputation that you didn't like? Did your family get angry with you?

   - *Step 2:* Explore general consequences for others. Say, "It is important to think ahead to consequences not only for you, but also to consequences for the other person, other people. In fact, we have a special name for it: TOP. TOP means 'think of the other person.' "

     Who, besides you, will be affected if you skip school? (parent, guardian, school staff)

     What hassles will your mom or dad have?

   - *Step 3:* Emphasize "feelings" consequences for others. Point out how the feelings of others are like those the group members have had—hurt, angry, upset, depressed, etc. Ask the following questions, then point out that, in a tiny way, your breaking the rules means the school is not the same anymore; the trust that is required for the school to function, one little piece of that trust for some people, has been destroyed.

     How will your mom or dad feel?

     Do you think they will ever be quite the same again?

     How will your mom or dad feel about telling close friends or your grandparents what happened?

     How will your grandparents feel—or the teachers who have helped you?

   - *Step 4:* Probe for "feelings" consequences to the rule breaker.

     How will you feel if you skip school—especially in those moments when you are not minimizing/mislabeling it as "no big deal"?

     How will you feel about having to lie to cover it up?

     When you honestly face up to it, do you think you'll feel bad about it, about how your actions harmed others and yourself?

     Have you had feelings like that before?

11. Conclude the meeting with the following:

As you can see, it is important to think ahead to all the kinds of consequences we have talked about. Before acting, it's important to think ahead to consequences for yourself, but it's also important to think ahead to consequences for others, to think "TOP," and to use the self-talk cues "check yourself," and "check your thoughts." It is very important to use these phrases to help yourself and others before a harmful act occurs. What might happen if you don't choose to check yourself or check your thoughts? *(Elicit the idea that sooner or later you may choose to break the rules or the law.)*

12. Tell participants the topic of the next meeting: using "I" statements for constructive consequences. Remind them to continue using their daily logs.

THINKING AHEAD TO CONSEQUENCES	Consequences for self	Consequences for others
General Consequences	Step 1	Step 2
"Feelings" Consequences	Step 4	Step 3

Session 6: Using "I" Statements for Constructive Consequences

Overview of activities

- Review of Session 5
- Understanding the consequences of anger
- Using "I" statements instead of "you" statements (put-downs and threats)
- Using "I" statements in the social skill Expressing a Complaint Constructively

Materials

- Daily logs (completed since the previous session)

Procedure

1. Use the Equipper's Guidelines from the previous session to review. Discuss participants' daily logs.

2. Review the anger "anatomy" learned so far:

   We've spent most of our time on the M in AMBC. We have also talked about the body reaction (B) and the activating event (A), or "hot spot."

   We said that the body that's getting angry is reacting to . . .What?

   Stress the point that mind activity is so crucial because the body reacts directly to that, not to the activating event. Review the meaning of C in AMBC (consequences) and remind participants that an angry mind and body will, if untreated with the techniques learned, lead sooner or later to destructive consequences. Say, "In other words, if you've allowed yourself to get too upset to think straight, then you're going to start to say or do some destructive things."

3. Explain that there are basically two kinds of destructive things you say when you're angry and out of control: put-downs and threats. Use the following example to illustrate.

   Let's say you loaned somebody your radio and now you want it back, and the person keeps not returning it, so when you see the person you say, "Hey, you jerk, you better give me back my radio if you know what's good for you!" In this case, what was the put-down? What was the threat?" (Discuss.)

4. Relate destructive consequences to "you" statements, and explain in contrast how "I" statements typically lead to more positive consequences:

   Put-downs and threats are "you" statements: "You jerk. You'd better do this or else." They are destructive because they attack the other person and provoke fights.

   Instead of being destructive, we want to be constructive, and we do this by replacing those "you" statements with "I" statements.

   Telling someone how you feel—for example, "I'm feeling pretty upset about this"—involves an "I" statement.

   An "I" statement makes a constructive suggestion: "I would like you to do this instead of that." "I" statements were part of a social skill we learned. Do you remember what social skill that was? (Expressing a Complaint Constructively; see Section 6.)

   If you've been using your anger reducers in hot spots, then you should be calm and straight thinking enough to express yourself in a calm, straightforward way. Is your tone of voice threatening when you express a complaint constructively? (Discuss the calm, constructive tone used in this skill.)

5. Remind participants that the skill involves three steps:

The first step is to state to yourself what the problem is, how you are feeling about it, and whether you are partly responsible for the problem.

The second step is to make plans for expressing your complaint, like deciding what person you were going to complain to and what you were going to say.

In the third step, you actually role-played Expressing a Complaint Constructively. And as a part of that step you told the person three things: (a) what the problem was, (b) how you felt about it, and (c) what you'd like done about it.

6. Give the following example:

If someone has borrowed your radio and still hasn't given it back, you can say, "I'm getting upset, Joe, because my radio was borrowed a while ago. I'd like to have it back now." What "I" statements do you hear there? *(Discuss calm, straightforward delivery.)*

What if you said, "I know I told you that you could keep it as long as you liked, but it turns out I miss it more than I thought." What's constructive about saying that? *(Discuss the value of showing that you understand the other person's point of view for encouraging the other person to listen to your point of view.)*

7. Point out that the strategy may not always work. So then what?

If the other person continues to violate your rights or ignores legitimate points, the nice thing about starting out low-key is that you still have room to gradually firm up your position—without becoming destructive.

You still don't threaten. But you do—in a calm, straightforward way—tell the other person what the consequences will be if the situation is not resolved satisfactorily.

If you say it in a menacing tone of voice, trying to use fear to get your way, you are being threatening, and the other person could be provoked into even worse actions. Besides, the person would probably like nothing better than to see you lose control.

To be effective, the consequence should be realistic—something you are willing to carry out. That's the difference between stating a consequence and making a threat.

8. Explain this difference as being the difference between staying calm and being angry, between saying something realistic and saying something crazy. For example, in the radio example, the situation could gradually escalate.

If you keep meeting with resistance after you've tried the calm, straightforward approach, you could say, "I want my radio now, please" or "I politely asked you to return my radio."

Finally with a calm, matter-of-fact tone of voice, state the consequence: "I will report to the staff that you have refused to return my radio."

Is that statement of consequence different from a threat? How? *(Discuss.)*

9. Summarize meeting content and let participants know the topic of the next meeting: self-evaluation. Remind them to continue using their daily logs.

Session 7: Self-Evaluation

Overview of activities

- Review of Session 6
- Self-evaluation statements (self-reward, constructive self-criticism)
- Self-evaluation and correction of thinking errors

Materials

- Participant Handout: Self-Talk Anger Reducers (from Session 2)
- Daily logs (completed since the last session)

Procedure

1. Use the Equipper's Guidelines to review Session 6, which focused on the way to achieve constructive consequences by replacing "you" statements (put-downs and threats) with "I" statements.

2. Introduce the main topic of the session, self-evaluation, and state that self-evaluation goes beyond consequences—it's something you should do after the consequences, after an incident is over one way or the other. Explain that self-evaluation is a very important activity and that participants should do it every day.

3. Go over the Self-Help Daily Log for Problems and Thinking Errors, emphasizing the link between good self-evaluations and positive self-talk:

   Where have you been rating yourself on this log? *(Discuss the anger and coping behavior evaluations.)*

   On this log, you did only number evaluations; however, you should do more than just that. If you gave yourself a 4 or a 5 ("well" or "great") for the way you handled yourself in a situation, then give yourself rewarding self-talk, a kind of mental pat on the back—like "Hey, I really kept cool" or "I handled that one pretty well" or "I'm doing better at this all the time." *(Refer as needed to the Participant Handout for Session 2, entitled "Self-Talk Anger Reducers.")*

   If you didn't handle the situation well, give yourself constructive feedback on what you can do to handle a situation better the next time—like "Next time I'll notice my early warning signs sooner, like my tense face or my angry self-talk."

   You may also need to tell yourself other constructive things, like what thinking errors you were making in the situation and what you need to tell yourself next time to talk back to those thinking errors.

4. Discuss how Gary, even after stabbing his girlfriend, could do a constructive self-evaluation and practice telling himself the truth so that he wouldn't hurt someone again. Say, "Don't mislabel yourself a failure if you don't control your anger perfectly. Instead, stay constructive. What can you do differently and how can you do better next time? Is there any technique you can use from what you've been learning in anger management?"

5. Explain that part of self-evaluation should be statements that sound something like this:

   "These are tough situations—they take time to learn how to straighten out."

   "I'll be better at this when I get more practice."

6. Summarize meeting content and let participants know the topic of the next meeting: reversing. Remind them to continue using their daily logs.

Session 8: Reversing

Overview of activities

- Review of Session 7

- Understanding things one does that make other people angry, realizing how one Aggravates Others (i.e., correcting for a Self-Centered tendency)

- Learning what to say when a group member makes a Blaming Others error

Materials

- Participant Handouts

  Things I Do to Aggravate Others

  Reversing

- Daily logs (completed since the last session)

Procedure

1. Use the Equipper's Guidelines from the previous meeting to review the last session's topic, self-evaluation. Discuss progress participants are making on their daily logs.

2. Explain that, during this session, you are going to take a slightly different angle on things:

   Up until this meeting, when we've talked about activating events, we've talked about the things other people do to make you angry, the hot spot you're in because of someone else's Aggravates Others problem.

   It was always that other person. But someone's got to be that other person, and most of us are that other person at least some of the time.

   So think about when *you're* that other person. In fact, if you're that other person a lot more often than you think, then what kind of thinking error are you making? *(Self-Centered)*

3. Discuss Self-Centered attitudes in terms of emphasizing others' roles in provocations but ignoring one's own. Remind the group of Gary and review how Gary ignored what he did to make his girl-friend, Cecelia, angry in the first place. Ask, "If you blame the other person when you should be at least partly blaming yourself, what kind of thinking error is that?" The answer, Blaming Others, should be fairly obvious.

4. Amplify the discussion of Blaming Others:

   You see, anger isn't just a problem of what others do to anger us and how we should reduce our anger and express a complaint constructively; it's also a problem because of things we do to make other people angry. We may tend to ignore the times we tease people or threaten them in some way or start rumors about them.

   That's why the self-help daily logs are important. The logs give you a chance to slow down, remember such times, and report when you've aggravated or otherwise harmed someone.

   So what do you do that amounts to someone else's activating event, someone else's hot spot? What have you done lately, or what did you do in the past? Look back at your daily logs, or ask the group.

5. Distribute copies of the Things I Do to Aggravate Others handout.

As with the self-evaluation that we learned about last week, the aim here is to be constructive. Once you're more aware of how you aggravate others—or how you're partly at fault when others are aggravating you—you're in a position to do something about it.

How did we say that Gary should talk back to his Self-Centered thinking error? *(Review Gary's taking his girlfriend's point of view and telling himself the truth: that she has a legitimate right to be upset and expect better treatment.)*

How did we say that Gary should talk back to his Blaming Others thinking error? *(Review Gary's telling himself the truth: that he started the provocations and that grabbing the knife was his choice.)*

6. Say, "Suppose a group member makes a Blaming Others thinking error, not silently but out loud. How would the group "talk back" to the group member to correct that Blaming Others thinking error? Distribute the Reversing handout and help the group process it:

The first three thinking error examples are answered for us. *(Discuss.)* What about the next one? What would you say? *(Read and discuss each subsequent example.)*

7. Summarize meeting content and let participants know the topic of the next meeting: more consequences for others and correcting distorted self-views. Remind them to continue using their daily logs.

Session 8: Things I Do to Aggravate Others

Name _____ Date _____

Describe two things you do that make other people angry or two things you have done that made someone else feel hurt or angry.

1. _____

_____

_____

_____

_____

_____

_____

_____

_____

2. _____

_____

_____

_____

_____

_____

_____

_____

_____

_____

Session 8: Reversing

Name _____ Date _____

1. The group member says: "I don't have any problem. You jerks are the ones with the problem, man. The only problem I have is you dummies keep hassling me, man.

   You say: "You know, it'll be great when you get the courage to face your problems. Then you'll thank people for trying to help you instead of putting them down and blaming them."

2. The group member says: "I got in trouble because both my parents are alcoholic and don't care about me."

   You say: "You mean that all people with parents who have problems go out and hurt people?"

3. The group member says: "It's all my mother's fault. They never would have caught me if she didn't tell the police I was stealing."

   You say: "Did your mother do the stealing? Did anybody force you to steal? No? So whose fault is it, really, that you're in trouble?"

4. The group member says: "My friends talked me into it—it's their fault. I just got mixed up with the wrong guys."

   You say:

   _____

   _____

   _____

5. The group member says: "I got in trouble because both my parents did drugs and neglected me."

   You say:

   _____

   _____

   _____

6. The group member says: "He was asking for it. He kept fooling around."

   You say:

   _____

   _____

   _____

7. The group member says: "The guy left his car unlocked. A fool like that deserved to get his car stolen."

   You say:

   _____

   _____

   _____

Session 9: More Consequences for Others/Correcting Distorted Self-Views

Overview of activities

- Review of Session 8

- Having empathy for victims and awareness of self as the one who has harmed innocent people

- Expanding the definition of TOP to include "Think of the pain your actions have caused other people"

Materials

- Participant Handouts

  Problem Names (from Section 3, pp. 19–21)

  Victims and Victimizers

- Daily logs (completed since the last session)

Procedure

1. Refer to the Equipper's Guidelines from the previous meeting to recap that session. Let the group know that this session will provide more ways to take the perspective of others—specifically, the perspectives of their victims. Review the group's use of the daily logs.

2. Introduce the following concepts:

   What is a victim? *(Define "victim" as someone who is unfairly hurt by someone else.)*

   What is a victimizer? *(Define "victimizer" as someone who hurts others, especially someone who unfairly hurts another person or people.)*

   We already have a good list of victimizing behaviors. *(Refer participants to the Problem Names handout.* Included on that list are some self-victimizing behaviors. Which ones are they?

   Pause for group members' responses and record them on the easel pad.

3. Distribute the Victims and Victimizers handout and encourage the group to discuss the questions presented there. Following are some special notes.

   - *Question 4:* This question is especially good for stimulating awareness of the permanent psychological harm that can result from victimization (some group members have explained articulately why getting insurance payments may not "make the situation all right" again).

   - *Question 5:* Consequences to victims are discussed systematically in this question. The discussion should be related to the idea of thinking ahead to consequences for others, presented in Session 5. For example:

     In body: Disfigured, bruised, broken bones, bloodied, heart attacks, loss of senses, beaten, raped

     In mind: Fear, apprehension, insecurity, loss of control over life, loss of concentration, confusion, thoughts of losing life, trauma, anxiety, irritability, guilt, grief over losing something personally meaningful, embarrassment, positive thoughts changing to negative thoughts, reliving of victimization, lack of trust, being emotionally guarded or paranoid, having uncontrollable emotions

     In money: Loss of job, unpaid bills, loss of money, cost to replace lost or damaged things, court costs, medical costs

     In daily living: Loss of sleep, disrupted schedule, can't get to work, loss of appetite, anxiety caused by red tape, increased stress/strain problems, health problems

     With friends: Isolated from others, teased or ignored by others, family problems

---

- *Question 7:* This question asks group members to apply their understanding of victimization to their personal circumstances and behavior. You can stress that although some victims do go on to be victimizers, many don't. You can also relate this question to TOP. Ask, "Remember TOP, from Session 5? Who remembers what TOP stands for?" Discuss how TOP—think of the other person— is informed by the previous list of ways victims suffer.

- *Question 8:* This question gives you the opportunity to ask group members whether their victims have suffered in some of the ways previously listed and to take responsibility for their own victimizing behavior.

4. Underscore the point that group members' own victimization does not mean that they have to victimize others; if that were true, then every victim would become a victimizer. Also point out that such an excuse is a Blaming Others thinking error: One is in effect blaming innocent people for what someone else did.

5. Continue expanding on the meaning of TOP:

TOP also stands for "think of the pain your actions have caused other people." This is self-evaluation on a big scale—evaluating your life, how you've harmed others, where you want to go from here. In the Alcoholics Anonymous 12-step program, this step is called "making a searching and fearless moral inventory."

Now instead of thinking ahead, you're thinking back. And that's the best way to think ahead to consequences for others: to think back to how your past irresponsible behavior has harmed them.

Imagine yourself as your victim—the pain, how it feels. Continue to think TOP, think of the other person and the pain you've caused, and stop yourself before you harm yourself or someone else again.

6. Share this example:

One man saved his life by using TOP.* He had a drinking problem and was about to backslide, to take another drink. Before he did, he thought about how when he was drinking he beat his wife and kids, and bought booze with the money his family desperately needed. His wife had left him. Now his wife was giving him another chance, trusting him to mean what he said about becoming responsible and helping his family. He was thinking ahead to what could happen if he took that drink. And he was thinking TOP. Do you think he took that drink? *(Discuss.)* That's right, he didn't.

7. Summarize meeting content and let participants know the topic of the next meeting: correction of distorted self-views and grand review. Remind them to continue using their daily logs.

---

*This example originally appeared in *The Criminal Personality: Vol. 3. The Drug User* (pp. 333–334) by S. Yochelson & S. E. Samenow, 1977, Northvale, NJ: Jason Aronson.

Session 9: Victims and Victimizers

Name _____ Date _____

You are attending a family wedding when you are asked to drive your grandparents home. Your grandparents have lived in that home for many years. You arrive home and help your grandparents into the house. When you open the front door, you see that the house has been broken into. Many of your grandparents' things have been thrown all around. Their crystal glasses have been smashed. The family photo album has been destroyed. Some of their things, like a wedding ring that belonged to your great grandmother, have been stolen.

1. What would be the first thing that you would do?

   _____

   _____

2. How do you think you would be feeling? Have you ever had anything stolen from you? How did you feel? Does that help you understand how your grandparents feel?

   _____

   _____

3. Would you leave your grandparents in the house alone for the night? Why or why not? Do you think your grandparents would feel afraid or worried? When have you felt afraid or worried? Does that help you understand how your grandparents would feel?

   _____

   _____

4. Do you think your grandparents will get their things back? Do you think the insurance (if they have any) can make the situation all right? Why or why not?

   _____

   _____

5. Who are the victims in this situation? Can you think of any long-term or indirect victims? List some ways that victims suffer (in body, in mind, in money, in daily living, with their friends).

   _____

   _____

6. Who are the main victimizers in this situation? If a victimizer were to think ahead to the many ways a victim would suffer, would he or she still go ahead and do the crime?

   _____

7. Have you been a victim? From whom? Have you victimized others? Whom have you victimized? Do most people who have been victimized go on to victimize others?

   _____

   _____

8. Which have you been more of, victim or victimizer?

   _____

   _____

Session 10: More Correction of Distorted Self-Views/Grand Review

Session goals

- Awareness of Self-Centered self-views
- Grand review
- Commitment to use the skills learned for managing anger and correcting thinking errors

Materials

- Participant Handout: The Mind of the Victimizer
- Daily logs (completed since the last session)

Procedure

1. Discuss group members' use of the daily logs, then review of the key points of the last meeting.

   The many ways in which acts of victimization harm others

   The fact that most victims are not, in turn, victimizers

   The error of thinking that having been a victim entitles one to victimize (Blaming Others)

   The acknowledgment by many group members that they have been victimizers more than victims

2. Lead the group to explore the mind of the victimizer more fully in order to understand what must change. Say, "Dr. Stanton Samenow is a psychologist who has studied and written about victimizers. He calls them criminals. He claims there is such a thing as a criminal mind—that is, because there is a criminal mind there is crime."

3. Distribute The Mind of the Victimizer handout to the group and explain that it was written by Dr. Samenow, but in this version the word *victimizer* has been substituted for the word *criminal*. Ask someone to read the initial quotation to the group, then have different group members read each question. Discuss each question in turn.

4. Conclude the session with a grand review of the key points of anger management.

   Session 1: The benefits of managing one's anger for gaining control and having behavioral options

   Session 2: The reaction of the body directly to the mind and only indirectly to the event

   Session 3: Using the example of the violence stemming from Gary's thinking errors to correct such errors

   Session 4: The use of anger reducers (calming and correcting self-talk, counting backwards, deep breathing, invoking peaceful imagery)

   Session 5: Thinking ahead to consequences (if-then thinking), think of the other person (TOP)

   Session 6: The use of "I" statements rather than "you" statements for constructive consequences

   Session 7: The role of self-evaluation

   Session 8: Understanding things one does that make other people angry (reversing), knowing how to "talk back" to others' Blaming Others thinking errors

   Session 9: The importance of telling oneself the truth about one's victimizing

5. Sum up this session's goal as helping participants recognize the need to make a commitment to develop, with the help of others, the mind and the life of a responsible person. Encourage participants to continue to use their daily logs.

Session 10: The Mind of a Victimizer

Name _____ Date _____

The victimizer believes he is entitled to whatever he desires. . . . Wherever the victimizer is—walking down the street, buying groceries at the supermarket, driving in rush hour traffic, riding the elevator to his apartment—he sees other people and property as opportunities for conquest. The sports car parked by the curb with the keys in the ignition could be his for the taking. The purse dangling from the super-market cart is a tempting target. The bank he passes looks like an easy hit. . . . Put a victimizer and a responsible person in the gift department of a department store and ask each as he comes out to recount his thoughts while there. The responsible person comments on the attractiveness, quality, and price of the merchandise, and perhaps on the efficiency of the service. In addition, he may describe a pretty sales-person or customer and recount a conversation overheard. The victimizer notices little of this. He deter-mines the best means to gain access to the merchandise as well as to customers' purses, wallets, and other personal belongings. He also notices the location of the cash register, the security arrangements, and the location of the nearest exit. In addition, he regards any attractive woman as his for the taking.

1. Do these words describe how you think when you are on the outside, as you are walking down the street, driving in a car, shopping in the supermarket or department store? What thinking error do the words describe? If you think like a victimizer, you will act like a victimizer.

   _____

   _____

   _____

2. In general, what has been your attitude toward other people and their property as you have gone through your life? How have you treated other people?

   _____

   _____

   _____

3. Most people want to be responsible, but some people don't care—they victimize others to get what they want. When a victimizer hurts a responsible person, how does the responsible person feel about the victimizer? In general, what should society do with victimizers?

   _____

   _____

   _____

   _____

4. Think about other people you have victimized, the suffering you have caused them—how do you feel? Do you want to change, to develop the mind and life of a responsible person? Can the group help you to change? Who has to make the choice to change, the effort to change?

   _____

   _____

   _____

   _____

Equipper's Review and Self-Evaluation Form:
Anger Management/Thinking Error Correction

Equipper _____ Date _____

Session/Skill _____ Group _____

In general

☐ yes ☐ no 1. Did group members follow the ground rules (concerning listening, confidentiality, etc.)?

☐ yes ☐ no 2. Were all group members interested and involved?

If no, list the names of uninvolved group members:

_____

_____

_____

☐ yes ☐ no 3. Did you find some constructive value in every serious comment made by a group member?

☐ yes ☐ no 4. Did you maintain a normal voice volume and speak in a respectful rather than threatening or demanding tone?

☐ yes ☐ no 5. Did you maintain a balance between criticism and approval by using the "sandwich" style of constructive criticism (in which a critical comment is preceded and followed by supportive ones)?

☐ yes ☐ no 6. Did you use the "ask, don't tell" intervention as much as possible?

For the session

Did you . . .

☐ yes ☐ no 1. *(After the first session)* Review the previous session's activities and go over participants' Self-Help Anger Logs?

☐ yes ☐ no 2. Use the discussion to continue clarifying the four thinking errors and the twelve social/behavioral problems (e.g., Easily Angered, Misleads Others, Lying)?

☐ yes ☐ no 3. Employ the easel pad to record the main points of the session and group member's responses?

☐ yes ☐ no 4. Remind group members to fill out the two daily logs: for problems and thinking errors and for positive behaviors?

☐ yes ☐ no 5. Keep the overall discussion a "step back" from the participants' personal problem/thinking error situations?

☐ yes ☐ no 6. Monitor/elicit/reward any recognition that anger is the product of one's thoughts?

☐ yes ☐ no 7. Monitor/elicit/reward the use of "self-talk" techniques?

☐ yes ☐ no 8. Monitor/elicit/reward recognition of the feelings of and/or harm done to another person?

SECTION SIX
Social Skills Training

INTRODUCTION

Social skills typically means balanced and constructive behavior in difficult interpersonal situations. An example is the behavior of a youth who deals constructively with deviant peer pressure by suggesting a responsible alternative, or one who calmly and sincerely offers clarification and/or apologizes to an angry accuser. One of us (Arnold P. Goldstein) has for many years made social skills easy to learn by breaking them down into manageable elements or "steps" (see Goldstein & McGinnis, 1997; McGinnis & Goldstein, 1997). Youths in an EQUIP program need to learn the steps of balanced and constructive social behavior if they are to be effective in helping themselves and fellow group members.

FORMAT OF THE SOCIAL SKILLS TRAINING MEETING
Introducing the Skill

1. Announce the social skill to be modeled and practiced.

2. If it is the group's first social skills training meeting, distribute and discuss the Social Skills Role-Playing handout.

3. Give each group member a copy of the Participant Handout for the specific skill.

4. Discuss situations in which the skill would be an important and useful tool.

5. Ask a group member to read the skill aloud.

Showing (Modeling) the Skill

1. Assign individual group members to give you feedback on each step of the skill you have chosen to model.

2. Show (model) the skill. If another actor is needed, ask for a volunteer or assign someone to assist you. You may have to coach your co-actor on his or her part.

3. After modeling the skill, ask the assigned students to give you their helpful feedback.

4. Model the proper way to accept feedback: by paying attention and thanking the students who give the feedback for providing it.

Trying the Skill

1. Ask for volunteers or assign group members to role-play the skill.

2. Ask for volunteers or assign specific group members to watch for and give feedback on how the role-player performs each step.

3. Facilitate the role-play.

4. Have other group members role-play the skill.

Discussing the Skill

1. Have the group members assigned to evaluate each step give their feedback. If needed, use "ask, don't tell" to solicit feedback from other group members (see pp. 29–32 of the EQUIP book).

2. During the discussion, make constructive interventions to maximize learning.

Practicing the Skill Outside the Meeting

1. Ask the group members to practice the skill outside the meeting.

2. Tell the group to use the Social Skills Practice form to record their practice between sessions.

ACTIVITIES AND MATERIALS

1. Be sure to read chapter 5 of the EQUIP book thoroughly before beginning social skills training meetings.

2. Before each meeting, photocopy enough Participant Handouts so every group member may have one. Optional: Before each session, write the skill steps on an easel pad and display it during the role-plays.

3. After each meeting, fill out the Equipper's Review and Self-Evaluation Form for social skills training.

   The materials for the Social Skills Training component are as follows:

   • *Social Skills Role-Playing.* A participant handout for the first meeting that briefly describes what is expected of participants.

   • *Social Skills Practice Form.* A form group members use to write down their social skills "homework assignment" and to record and report on the outcome of this practice.

   • *Participant Handouts.* One per skill, separate handouts detailing the behavioral steps in each skill and including a list of situations in which the skill would be useful.

   • *Equipper's Guidelines.* Reproductions of the skill steps and situations from Participant Handouts, plus additional comments and questions to help guide discussion. In these guidelines, notes to equippers appear in italics.

Social Skills Role-Playing

Name _____ Date _____

Role-playing a social skill is the same as rehearsing for a play or running drills with a band or sports team. To have a "good show" or a "winning team," you have to practice, and you have to be serious about the practice. Even though it is serious it can still be fun, just like the play, band, or team is fun. The fun is in improving your relationships with other people and feeling good about it. Go for it!

1. Think of a situation or select one from the list on your Participant Handout.

2. Pick out partner(s) for your role-play. Your partner(s) are group members who work with you toward a successful role-play. The partner(s) job is to be helpful and realistic in acting out the situation. The equipper can help you and your partner(s) decide how to act.

3. To set up the role-play, explain the situation to your partner and then to the group.

4. Ask the other group members to give you feedback on how well you do on each of the skill steps.

5. Role-play the skill with your partner(s). Think *aloud* about the situation and the skill steps.

6. Listen to the feedback from group members.

7. Thank them and, if needed, say how you could change what you did to improve your use of the skill.

Social Skills Practice Form

Name _____ Date _____

Fill in during this meeting

1. Practice assignment

   a. Skill

   If applicable:

   b. Use with whom

   c. Use when

   d. Use where

Fill in before next meeting

2. Describe what happened when you did the practice assignment. For example, did you skip any steps? What was the other person's reaction?

3. Rate yourself on how well you used the skill. *(Check one.)*

   ☐ excellent   ☐ good   ☐ fair   ☐ poor

Skill 1: Expressing a Complaint Constructively

> Before you start, pick a partner and discuss your role-play. Follow the steps to help you describe your situation to the group.

Step 1: Identify the problem

How are you feeling? What is the problem? Who is responsible for it? Did you contribute—or are you contributing—to the problem in any way?

Discuss how you can recognize a problem—by how the person treats you or what he or she says to you; by the way you act toward someone or what you say to them; by the way you feel inside.

Step 2: Plan and think ahead

To whom should you express your complaint? When? Where? What will you say? (See Step 3.)

Discuss when is a good time to tell that person—when the person isn't involved with something else, when the person is alone and seems calm. Advise participants to wait until they have calmed down before approaching the person.

> For Steps 3 and 4, you will need your partner.

Step 3: State your complaint

Greet the person in a friendly way. Calmly and straightforwardly, tell the person the problem and how you feel about it. If you've contributed to the problem, mention how you may be partly at fault and what *you* are willing to do.

Point out that if the person gets angry, you can talk about the problem some other time. The person is less likely to get angry if you are strong enough to apologize for your role in the problem.

Step 4: Make a constructive suggestion

Tell the person what you would like done about the problem. Ask the other person if he or she thinks your suggestion is fair. If the other person makes a constructive suggestion, say that you appreciate the suggestion or that it sounds fair.

Participants can mention how their suggestion would help the other person, too. To help clear up any remaining hard feelings, participants may wish to ask the person how he or she feels about the suggestion.

Suggested situations for using this skill

1. The teacher gives you an assignment that seems too difficult for you.
2. Your parents won't let you go to a movie with a friend.
3. Your friend usually chooses what the two of you will do.
4. Your friend has spread a rumor about you.
5. You are always doing the hardest work in the kitchen.
6. None of the other workers is helping you out.
7. You just bought a pair of sneakers and left the store, and now you realize the salesperson short-changed you.
8. You just found out who stole your sneakers.
9. You share a room at home with your brother, who is always using your things without asking you.
10. You are having lunch at the facility, and you just took the first bite of your sandwich. Something tastes really spoiled.

11. You are being restricted for being disrespectful. You feel that the staff provoked you and that the restriction is unfair.

12. Your teacher keeps giving you work that is too easy. It's the same work over and over again, and you are really bored.

13. Your counselor always seems to have time to talk with the other youth in your group but never seems to have time to talk with you.

14. At home, your mother always wants you in by 10:30 P.M., but you don't want to come home that early.

Skill 1: Expressing a Complaint Constructively

Name _____ Date _____

> Before you start, pick a partner and discuss your role-play. Follow the
> steps to help you describe your situation to the group.

Step 1: Identify the problem

How are you feeling? What is the problem? Who is responsible for it? Did you contribute—or are you contributing—to the problem in any way?

Step 2: Plan and think ahead

To whom should you express your complaint? When? Where? What will you say? (See Step 3.)

> For Steps 3 and 4, you will need your partner.

Step 3: State your complaint

Greet the person in a friendly way. Calmly and straightforwardly, tell the person the problem and how you feel about it. If you've contributed to the problem, mention how you may be partly at fault and what *you* are willing to do.

Step 4: Make a constructive suggestion

Tell the person what you would like done about the problem. Ask the other person if he or she thinks your suggestion is fair. If the other person makes a constructive suggestion, say that you appreciate the suggestion or that it sounds fair.

Suggested situations for using this skill

1. The teacher gives you an assignment that seems too difficult for you.
2. Your parents won't let you go to a movie with a friend.
3. Your friend usually chooses what the two of you will do.
4. Your friend has spread a rumor about you.
5. You are always doing the hardest work in the kitchen.
6. None of the other workers is helping you out.
7. You just bought a pair of sneakers and left the store, and now you realize the salesperson short-changed you.
8. You just found out who stole your sneakers.
9. You share a room at home with your brother, who is always using your things without asking you.
10. You are having lunch at the facility, and you just took the first bite of your sandwich. Something tastes really spoiled.
11. You are being restricted for being disrespectful. You feel that the staff provoked you and that the restriction is unfair.
12. Your teacher keeps giving you work that is too easy. It's the same work over and over again, and you are really bored.
13. Your counselor always seems to have time to talk with the other youth in your group but never seems to have time to talk with you.
14. At home, your mother always wants you in by 10:30 P.M., but you don't want to come home that early.

Skill 1: Expressing a Complaint Constructively

Skill 2: Caring for Someone Who Is Sad or Upset

> Before you start, pick a partner and discuss your role-play. Follow the
> steps to help you describe your situation to the group.

Step 1: Watch the person (but don't stare)

Does he or she look or sound sad? Upset? How strong might the feelings be?

Participants will need to pay attention to signs that the person may be sad or upset: hunched-over posture, expression on face, tone of voice. (Maybe you know something about what's troubling the person, maybe you don't.)

Step 2: Plan and think ahead

Ask yourself, "Should I walk over to the person? Now? Or later?"

Emphasize that if the person seems very angry or upset, it may be best to wait until the person has calmed down.

> For Steps 3 and 4, you will need your partner.

Step 3: Start a conversation

Walk over to the person. Say something like "What's up?" "How are you feeling?" or "Want to talk about it?"

Step 4: Listen and "be there"

Listen to what the person says. Encourage him or her to talk. Say something like "So you're kinda bummed out." After the person seems done for the time, say something like "I'll be around if you want to talk some more about it" or "Let me know if there's anything I can do."

Participants should not interrupt unless it's to encourage the person to say more. Stress that listening is very important: Do not start giving advice right away, or maybe don't give it at all. It may be proper just to listen.

Suggested situations for using this skill

1. A neighbor's family member has been ill.
2. Your dad or mom is slamming doors and muttering to himself/herself.
3. A friend hasn't been chosen for a game, or a classmate just watches a game instead of asking to join.
4. An old friend of yours tells you that he has just received a letter from his girlfriend, and she has broken up with him.
5. A friend has just told you that his brand-new sneakers have been stolen.
6. A youth you know in another unit is upset because her parents, who have promised to visit for the last 3 weeks, have not shown up.
7. The new person in your unit is homesick.
8. A neighbor who is a good friend of yours tells you that he has just learned that his girlfriend is pregnant.
9. A youth in your unit has just told the unit that his mother died of cancer last night.
10. Your sister just failed her G.E.D. exam.
11. Your closest friend just found out that his parents are getting separated.

Skill 2: Caring for Someone Who Is Sad or Upset

Name _____ Date _____

> Before you start, pick a partner and discuss your role-play. Follow the steps to help you describe your situation to the group.

Step 1: Watch the person (but don't stare)
Does he or she look or sound sad? Upset? How strong might the feelings be?

Step 2: Plan and think ahead
Ask yourself, "Should I walk over to the person? Now? Or later?"

> For Steps 3 and 4, you will need your partner.

Step 3: Start a conversation
Walk over to the person. Say something like "What's up?" "How are you feeling?" or "Want to talk about it?"

Step 4: Listen and "be there"
Listen to what the person says. Encourage him or her to talk. Say something like "So you're kinda bummed out." After the person seems done for the time, say something like "I'll be around if you want to talk some more about it" or "Let me know if there's anything I can do."

Suggested situations for using this skill

1. A neighbor's family member has been ill.

2. Your dad or mom is slamming doors and muttering to himself/herself.

3. A friend hasn't been chosen for a game, or a classmate just watches a game instead of asking to join.

4. An old friend of yours tells you that he has just received a letter from his girlfriend, and she has broken up with him.

5. A friend has just told you that his brand-new sneakers have been stolen.

6. A youth you know in another unit is upset because her parents, who have promised to visit for the last 3 weeks, have not shown up.

7. The new person in your unit is homesick.

8. A neighbor who is a good friend of yours tells you that he has just learned that his girlfriend is pregnant.

9. A youth in your unit has just told the unit that his mother died of cancer last night.

10. Your sister just failed her G.E.D. exam.

11. Your closest friend just found out that his parents are getting separated.

Skill 3: Dealing Constructively with Negative Peer Pressure

Ask participants to describe an original situation, or use one of the suggested situations. Have the participants start role-playing the skill, then freeze the role-play after the negative pressure has been established. Discuss the skill steps, then resume the role-play. Have only the participant dealing with the pressure follow the steps.

> For this role-play, you will choose one or more partners. Follow the
> instructions your equipper gives you.

Step 1: Think, "Why?"

Think about what the other person or persons are saying. What is it they want you to do? Why do they want you to do it?

Step 2: Think ahead

Think about the consequences if you do what they want you to do. Who might get hurt? How might you feel if you go along? How *should* you feel if you go along?

> For Steps 3 and 4, you will need your partner.

Step 3: Decide what you should do

What reasons will you give the person or persons? (This will help with Step 4.) What will you suggest to do instead? (This will help with Step 5.)

Instruct the co-actors to rejoin the role-play.

Step 4: Tell

In a calm, straightforward way, tell one of the persons what you have decided. Give a good reason—for example, how the pressure makes you feel or who might get hurt if you do what they want.

Encourage the role-player to tell his or her decision to one person only. Giving a good reason for not going along may help the group rethink what they should do.

Step 5: Suggest something else to do

This could be something responsible but still enjoyable.

Point out that this social skill is a good tool for helping group members with an Easily Misled problem. It is also important to stress that blaming irresponsible behavior on negative peer pressure involves a Blaming Others thinking error.

Suggested situations for using this skill

1. A group is teasing someone or planning to take something that belongs to someone else, and they want you to go along with them.

2. A group is planning to vandalize a neighborhood and wants you to come along.

3. Three friends just asked you to run away with them.

4. Several members of your unit tell you that they're going to steal cigarettes from a staff member, and they want you to be the lookout.

5. You've just been released home, and it's your first week in school. Some of your old friends have decided that they are going to skip a day and not go to school. They have just asked you to come with them.

6. Three friends pull over in a car you think they may have stolen. They ask you to get in and go for a ride.

7. You are at a party at a friend's house and some of the other guys ask you to help search for any liquor in the house.

8. An old friend of yours has just asked you to join him and another friend in snatching a purse from an old lady who is walking down the street.

Skill 3: Dealing Constructively with Negative Peer Pressure

Name _____ Date _____

> For this role-play, you will choose one or more partners. Follow the
> instructions your equipper gives you.

Step 1: Think, "Why?"

Think about what the other person or persons are saying. What is it they want you to do? Why do they want you to do it?

Step 2: Think ahead

Think about the consequences if you do what they want you to do. Who might get hurt? How might you feel if you go along? How *should* you feel if you go along?

> For Steps 3 and 4, you will need your partner.

Step 3: Decide what you should do

What reasons will you give the person or persons? (This will help with Step 4.) What will you suggest to do instead? (This will help with Step 5.)

Step 4: Tell

In a calm, straightforward way, tell one of the persons what you have decided. Give a good reason—for example, how the pressure makes you feel or who might get hurt if you do what they want.

Step 5: Suggest something else to do

This could be something responsible but still enjoyable.

Suggested situations for using this skill

1. A group is teasing someone or planning to take something that belongs to someone else, and they want you to go along with them.

2. A group is planning to vandalize a neighborhood and wants you to come along.

3. Three friends just asked you to run away with them.

4. Several members of your unit tell you that they're going to steal cigarettes from a staff member, and they want you to be the lookout.

5. You've just been released home, and it's your first week in school. Some of your old friends have decided that they are going to skip a day and not go to school. They have just asked you to come with them.

6. Three friends pull over in a car you think they may have stolen. They ask you to get in and go for a ride.

7. You are at a party at a friend's house and some of the other guys ask you to help search for any liquor in the house.

8. An old friend of yours has just asked you to join him and another friend in snatching a purse from an old lady who is walking down the street.

Skill 4: Keeping Out of Fights

> Before you start, pick a partner and discuss your role-play. Follow the steps to help you describe your situation to the group.

Step 1: Stop and think about why you want to fight

Tell participants that if they need to, they can breathe deeply, count backward, or think relaxing thoughts to calm down. They can also consider whether or not they did anything to contribute to the problem.

Step 2: Think ahead

Ask yourself, "If I fight, then what will be the consequences?"

Encourage participants to think about consequences for others, including people who are not on the scene but who will be affected later on. Ask, "How will they feel?"; "What will they do?"; "How will you feel?"; "What are the likely consequences later on for you?"

> For Step 3, you will need your partner.

Step 3: Think of a way to handle the situation besides fighting and do it

Should you walk away for now? Give a displeased look? Talk to the person in a calm, straightforward way? Ask someone for help in solving the problem?

Discuss: "Is the other person calm enough or reasonable enough to talk to? Are you calm enough yet to talk to? Who might be able to help you resolve the situation constructively (teacher, parent, friends)?" Point out that in some situations, such as self-defense or the defense of an innocent victim, you may have no choice but to fight.

Suggested situations for using this skill

1. Another youth has just come up to you and demanded that you give him cigarettes.
2. You just found out who stole your sneakers.
3. Another youth has just bumped into you and made you spill your drink and drop your food tray on the floor.
4. Another resident has just directed a racial slur at you.
5. Another resident tells you she has rights to the chair you are sitting on.
6. You lost your privileges because someone told your counselor that you were smoking cigarettes in the bathroom, and you just found out who told.
7. A resident to whom you loaned a pack of cigarettes is now refusing to pay you back.
8. Your mother's boyfriend is drunk and getting a little nasty.
9. A new resident comes up to you and calls you a name.
10. In a baseball game, you have just come up to bat. The other team's pitcher calls you a name and almost hits you with a pitch.

Skill 4: Keeping Out of Fights

Name _____ Date _____

> Before you start, pick a partner and discuss your role-play. Follow the steps to help you describe your situation to the group.

Step 1: Stop and think about why you want to fight

Step 2: Think ahead

Ask yourself, "If I fight, then what will be the consequences?"

> For Step 3, you will need your partner.

Step 3: Think of a way to handle the situation besides fighting and do it

Should you walk away for now? Give a displeased look? Talk to the person in a calm, straightforward way? Ask someone for help in solving the problem?

Suggested situations for using this skill

1. Another youth has just come up to you and demanded that you give him cigarettes.

2. You just found out who stole your sneakers.

3. Another youth has just bumped into you and made you spill your drink and drop your food tray on the floor.

4. Another resident has just directed a racial slur at you.

5. Another resident tells you she has rights to the chair you are sitting on.

6. You lost your privileges because someone told your counselor that you were smoking cigarettes in the bathroom, and you just found out who told.

7. A resident to whom you loaned a pack of cigarettes is now refusing to pay you back.

8. Your mother's boyfriend is drunk and getting a little nasty.

9. A new resident comes up to you and calls you a name.

10. In a baseball game, you have just come up to bat. The other team's pitcher calls you a name and almost hits you with a pitch.

Skill 5: Helping Others

Before you start, pick a partner and discuss your role-play. Follow the steps to help you describe your situation to the group.

Step 1: Think, "Is there a need?"

Decide if the other person might need or want your help.

Tell the group to think really hard about the needs of the other person: What is the person doing or saying, or what is happening, that makes you think the person needs help?

Step 2: Think of the ways you could be helpful

Which way would be best?

Encourage participants to ask, "Does the person need something done? Need someone to listen? Need to hear words of encouragement? Should someone else help?"

Step 3: Plan and think ahead

Ask yourself, "Is this a good time to offer help?"

Participants should ask themselves whether the person could use the help better later. If so, they will need to be sure they are not supposed to be doing something else at the time they offer help.

For Step 4, you will need your partner.

Step 4: Offer to help

Ask the other person, "Need some help?" or "Want some help?" or go ahead and offer to help in some way. If the other person is agreeable, continue with the help.

Emphasize that it is important to make the offer sincerely, allowing the other person to say no if he or she does not really want help. Point out that participants should not feel hurt or offended if the person says no or asks someone else for help. If they do help, they should ask themselves how they feel when they help others. When they are being helped? Point out that helping others is what the program is all about.

It is important to help the youth to understand that helping people sometimes means doing something against their wishes—for example, saying no if a person wants them to get drugs or harm someone.

Suggested situations for using this skill

1. Your friend has a drinking problem.

2. A sick friend needs to keep up-to-date with schoolwork.

3. The person who is sitting next to you in math class is having trouble understanding the assignment.

4. You are walking down the street and see a lady standing beside her car, which has a flat tire.

5. Two unit members got into a dumb argument, and now it looks as though they are about to get into a fight neither of them wants.

6. A friend of yours wants to go to the movies but doesn't have enough money.

7. Your teacher needs help arranging chairs in the classroom.

8. Your brother is probably not going to finish his chores in time to leave for a date.

Skill 5: Helping Others

Name _____ Date _____

> Before you start, pick a partner and discuss your role-play. Follow the
> steps to help you describe your situation to the group.

Step 1: Think, "Is there a need?"
Decide if the other person might need or want your help.

Step 2: Think of the ways you could be helpful
Which way would be best?

Step 3: Plan and think ahead
Ask yourself, "Is this a good time to offer help?"

> For Step 4, you will need your partner.

Step 4: Offer to help
Ask the other person, "Need some help?" or "Want some help?" or go ahead and offer to help in some way. If the other person is agreeable, continue with the help.

Suggested situations for using this skill

1. Your friend has a drinking problem.

2. A sick friend needs to keep up-to-date with schoolwork.

3. The person who is sitting next to you in math class is having trouble understanding the assignment.

4. You are walking down the street and see a lady standing beside her car, which has a flat tire.

5. Two unit members got into a dumb argument, and now it looks as though they are about to get into a fight neither of them wants.

6. A friend of yours wants to go to the movies but doesn't have enough money.

7. Your teacher needs help arranging chairs in the classroom.

8. Your brother is probably not going to finish his chores in time to leave for a date.

Skill 6: Preparing for a Stressful Conversation

> You do not need a partner for this role-play. Follow the steps to help you describe your situation to the group.

Step 1: Imagine yourself in the stressful situation

How will you feel at the start of the stressful situation? Who is responsible for the situation?

Participants might feel tense, anxious, defensive, impatient, and so on.

Step 2: Imagine the other person in the stressful situation

How might the other person feel at the start of the stressful situation? Why?

Relate this to TOP self-talk. (See the EQUIP book, pp. 143–147, and pp. 61–63 in this guide.)

Step 3: Plan what to say

Practice saying it in a calm, straightforward way.

Tell group members that if they can think of any way they have contributed to the stressful situation, they can mention that while practicing saying what they want to say.

Step 4: Think ahead to how the other person might feel

What might he or she say in response to what you will say?

Ask participants, "Will the other person respond constructively to what you plan to say? If not, can you think of anything better to say?"

Suggested situations for using this skill

Preparing to ask for something important or to seek some important goal in the conversation

1. You have an appointment tomorrow to talk to your school's football coach about trying out for the team. He is known to be a very tough guy.

2. You have a job interview with the facility's vocational specialist at 2:00 P.M.

3. You want to ask a person you like for a first date.

4. You need to talk to your teacher about your wish to drop a subject.

Preparing to reveal or explain something upsetting to someone

5. You prepare to tell your parent about a school failure.

6. You have been caught smoking a joint, and you know you will have to speak about it to your counselor, who is coming in on the next shift.

7. You have to go talk to a staff person, your teacher, to discuss an earlier incident in which you have been disrespectful and have cursed at her.

8. You have to talk to the facility nurse (or to your partner) and say that you think you may have a sexually transmitted disease.

9. You have to telephone your parent this afternoon and say that you got into a fight, so the parole board may hold you for several months.

10. You are sitting outside the facility director's office, waiting to talk about your escape attempt last night.

Skill 6: Preparing for a Stressful Conversation

Name _____ Date _____

> You do not need a partner for this role-play. Follow the steps to help you describe your situation to the group.

Step 1: Imagine yourself in the stressful situation
How will you feel at the start of the stressful situation? Who is responsible for the situation?

Step 2: Imagine the other person in the stressful situation
How might the other person feel at the start of the stressful situation? Why?

Step 3: Plan what to say
Practice saying it in a calm, straightforward way.

Step 4: Think ahead to how the other person might feel
What might he or she say in response to what you will say?

Suggested situations for using this skill

Preparing to ask for something important or to seek some important goal in the conversation

1. You have an appointment tomorrow to talk to your school's football coach about trying out for the team. He is known to be a very tough guy.

2. You have a job interview with the facility's vocational specialist at 2:00 P.M.

3. You want to ask a person you like for a first date.

4. You need to talk to your teacher about your wish to drop a subject.

Preparing to reveal or explain something upsetting to someone

5. You prepare to tell your parent about a school failure.

6. You have been caught smoking a joint, and you know you will have to speak about it to your counselor, who is coming in on the next shift.

7. You have to go talk to a staff person, your teacher, to discuss an earlier incident in which you have been disrespectful and have cursed at her.

8. You have to talk to the facility nurse (or to your partner) and say that you think you may have a sexually transmitted disease.

9. You have to telephone your parent this afternoon and say that you got into a fight, so the parole board may hold you for several months.

10. You are sitting outside the facility director's office, waiting to talk about your escape attempt last night.

Skill 7: Dealing Constructively with Someone Angry at You

To make this role-play more realistic, have several group members at once play the angry role and/or have several other group members "pump up" the role-player.

> Before you start, pick a partner and discuss your role-play. Follow the steps to help you describe your situation to the group.

Step 1: Listen openly and patiently to what the other person is saying

Nod your head or say "mm-hmm." If you need to, ask the angry person to tell you specifically what things you said or did that made him or her upset.

Stress that it is important not to interrupt or fidget. If group members feel themselves getting angry, they can breathe deeply or tell themselves to stay calm. Ask them to put themselves in the angry person's place (TOP) and remember that defending themselves at this point will only make the person angrier.

Step 2: Tell the person you understand why he or she is upset or that he or she has a right to be angry

Think of something you can agree with—say that the person is right about that.

If participants can't agree with any part of what the person is saying, they can agree that they do sometimes make mistakes or hurt people and that they regret this when it happens.

Step 3: Apologize or explain

Make a constructive suggestion to correct the problem.

Tell participants that if they are mainly at fault, then they will need to apologize for the hurt they caused and say that they plan to do better (and mean it!).

Suggested situations for using this skill

1. Your teacher is angry with you because you were disruptive during class.

2. Your parent is angry about the mess you've left the house in.

3. Your friend is angry about the fact that you called him a name.

4. A youth in your unit is angry because you cut in front in the dinner line.

5. It is 2:00 A.M., and you have just arrived home. Your parent is very angry because you were supposed to be home no later than 10:30 P.M.

6. A youth in your group has just gotten heavily sanctioned. You started the fight that made this happen, and the person is very angry with you.

7. Some of the members of your team are angry because you fouled an opposing player, the player scored, and your team lost the basketball game.

8. The cook who is serving the food is angry with you because she just heard you tell another person how bad it tasted.

9. A student threatens you and the rest of your unit, saying she'll get even with the person who took her snack.

Skill 7: Dealing Constructively with Someone Angry at You

Name _____ Date _____

> Before you start, pick a partner and discuss your role-play. Follow the steps to help you describe your situation to the group.

Step 1: Listen openly and patiently to what the other person is saying

Nod your head or say "mm-hmm." If you need to, ask the angry person to tell you specifically what things you said or did that made him or her upset.

Step 2: Tell the person you understand why he or she is upset or that he or she has a right to be angry

Think of something you can agree with—say that the person is right about that.

Step 3: Apologize or explain

Make a constructive suggestion to correct the problem.

Suggested situations for using this skill

1. Your teacher is angry with you because you were disruptive during class.

2. Your parent is angry about the mess you've left the house in.

3. Your friend is angry about the fact that you called him a name.

4. A youth in your unit is angry because you cut in front in the dinner line.

5. It is 2:00 A.M., and you have just arrived home. Your parent is very angry because you were supposed to be home no later than 10:30 P.M.

6. A youth in your group has just gotten heavily sanctioned. You started the fight that made this happen, and the person is very angry with you.

7. Some of the members of your team are angry because you fouled an opposing player, the player scored, and your team lost the basketball game.

8. The cook who is serving the food is angry with you because she just heard you tell another person how bad it tasted.

9. A student threatens you and the rest of your unit, saying she'll get even with the person who took her snack.

Skill 8: Expressing Care and Appreciation

> Before you start, pick a partner and discuss your role-play. Follow the steps to help you describe your situation to the group.

Step 1: Think, "Would the other person like to know that you care about and appreciate him or her?"
How will the person feel?

Explain that the other person may become embarrassed or may feel good.

Step 2: Plan and think ahead
What will you say? When and where will you say it?

Point out that it is often easier to express care and appreciation when others aren't around.

> For Step 3, you will need your partner.

Step 3: Tell the person how you feel in a friendly manner

Suggested situations for using this skill

1. You thank a teacher for something he or she has done.

2. You tell your parents that you love them.

3. You tell your friends that you like them and want to continue being friends.

4. Your counselor or group member has helped you work out a serious problem.

5. You have been on the unit for about 45 days. Your parents have just arrived for their first visit. You are really excited about seeing them.

6. You have really made a lot of progress in your reading, and it's time for you to be released from the program. You must say good-bye to your reading teacher.

7. Your partner has just told you over the phone that he or she loves you.

8. You are on emergency home leave because your grandmother, who has spent the most time raising you, is very sick. You are visiting her in the hospital.

9. Your little brother, who is 10 years old, is getting high every day. You really care for him a lot.

10. You are leaving the facility after a year and have to say good-bye to another resident, who has become the best friend you ever had.

11. It is your first week home after being released from the facility. You have not seen your best and oldest friend for a year, and now you spot your friend walking toward you on the street.

12. Your mother has just given you a new coat for your birthday.

Skill 8: Expressing Care and Appreciation

Name _____ Date _____

> Before you start, pick a partner and discuss your role-play. Follow the steps to help you describe your situation to the group.

Step 1: Think, "Would the other person like to know that you care about and appreciate him or her?"
How will the person feel?

Step 2: Plan and think ahead
What will you say? When and where will you say it?
Point out that it is often easier to express care and appreciation when others aren't around.

> For Step 3, you will need your partner.

Step 3: Tell the person how you feel in a friendly manner

Suggested situations for using this skill

1. You thank a teacher for something he or she has done.

2. You tell your parents that you love them.

3. You tell your friends that you like them and want to continue being friends.

4. Your counselor or group member has helped you work out a serious problem.

5. You have been on the unit for about 45 days. Your parents have just arrived for their first visit. You are really excited about seeing them.

6. You have really made a lot of progress in your reading, and it's time for you to be released from the program. You must say good-bye to your reading teacher.

7. Your partner has just told you over the phone that he or she loves you.

8. You are on emergency home leave because your grandmother, who has spent the most time raising you, is very sick. You are visiting her in the hospital.

9. Your little brother, who is 10 years old, is getting high every day. You really care for him a lot.

10. You are leaving the facility after a year and have to say good-bye to another resident, who has become the best friend you ever had.

11. It is your first week home after being released from the facility. You have not seen your best and oldest friend for a year, and now you spot your friend walking toward you on the street.

12. Your mother has just given you a new coat for your birthday.

Skill 9: Dealing Constructively with Someone Accusing You of Something

> Before you start, pick a partner and discuss your role-play. Follow the steps to help you describe your situation to the group.

Step 1: Think, "How do I feel?"

If you are upset, stop and say to yourself, "I have to calm down."

If necessary, group members can also take a deep breath or count to 10. If the other person is very angry, they can tell the person that they understand how he or she feels, or that he or she has a right to be upset.

Step 2: Think, "What is the other person accusing me of?"

Is he or she right?

Explain that it is important to be honest with yourself about the situation. (This step amounts to using TOP.)

> For Step 3, you will need your partner.

Step 3

If the accuser is right: In a calm, straightforward way, say you're sorry

Offer to make up for what happened, or say you are sorry and won't do it again.

If the accuser is wrong: In a calm, straightforward way, tell the accuser that what he or she said isn't true or that you didn't do it

You may mention that you're sorry the person got the wrong impression, that this is a lot of false talk, or that you would like an apology.

Stress the importance of being sincere, not "slick." Remind participants that anger reducers such as calming self-talk, deep breathing, and counting backward are helpful when using this skill.

Suggested situations for using this skill

1. A teacher has accused you of cheating.
2. Your parent accuses you of breaking something.
3. A friend accuses you of taking something of hers.
4. A neighbor accuses you of breaking his window.
5. Your parent accuses you of having hurt your sibling's feelings with your remark.
6. A friend accuses you of having lied.
7. A store owner accuses you of taking a new pair of pants from the store.
8. Your teacher accuses you of being lazy and never finishing your work.
9. Your counselor accuses you of always getting others to do your dirty work for you.
10. Your friends accuse you of always thinking of yourself first.
11. Your father accuses you of taking money from his wallet.
12. Your mother accuses you of being just like your father, a no-good bum.

Skill 9: Dealing Constructively with Someone Accusing You of Something

Name _____ Date _____

> Before you start, pick a partner and discuss your role-play. Follow the
> steps to help you describe your situation to the group.

Step 1: Think, "How do I feel?"

If you are upset, stop and say to yourself, "I have to calm down."

Step 2: Think, "What is the other person accusing me of?"

Is he or she right?

> For Step 3, you will need your partner.

Step 3

If the accuser is right: In a calm, straightforward way, say you're sorry

Offer to make up for what happened, or say you are sorry and won't do it again.

If the accuser is wrong: In a calm, straightforward way, tell the accuser that what he or she said isn't true or that you didn't do it

You may mention that you're sorry the person got the wrong impression, that this is a lot of false talk, or that you would like an apology.

Suggested situations for using this skill

1. A teacher has accused you of cheating.

2. Your parent accuses you of breaking something.

3. A friend accuses you of taking something of hers.

4. A neighbor accuses you of breaking his window.

5. Your parent accuses you of having hurt your sibling's feelings with your remark.

6. A friend accuses you of having lied.

7. A store owner accuses you of taking a new pair of pants from the store.

8. Your teacher accuses you of being lazy and never finishing your work.

9. Your counselor accuses you of always getting others to do your dirty work for you.

10. Your friends accuse you of always thinking of yourself first.

11. Your father accuses you of taking money from his wallet.

12. Your mother accuses you of being just like your father, a no-good bum.

Skill 10: Responding Constructively to Failure

This skill is an important tool for helping a young person with a Low Self-Image problem and/or an Assuming the Worst thinking error.

> You do not need a partner for this role-play. Follow the steps to help you describe your situation to the group.

Step 1: Ask yourself, "Did I fail?"

Decide if you have failed.

Explain that there is a difference between failing and not doing quite as well as you hoped.

Step 2: Ask yourself, "Why did I fail?"

Think about both the thinking errors and the circumstances that contributed to your failure.

Ask, "Did you not try as hard as you could have? Did you have an overconfident or Self-Centered attitude? Were you ready? Was the task too complicated for you, or were you just unlucky?" Encourage group members to avoid Assuming the Worst.

Step 3: Think about what you could do differently next time

Ask, "Could you practice more? Change your attitude or way of thinking? Try harder? Ask for help?"

Step 4: Decide if you want to try again or get another chance and do better

Step 5: If appropriate, make a plan to try again

Remember how you can do things differently.

Encourage group members to write down their plans. Stress that "plan" is another way of saying, "Think ahead."

Suggested situations for using this skill

1. You failed a test at school.

2. You failed to complete your chores at home.

3. You failed to get the group to do the activity you wanted to do.

4. You spent 3 weeks trying to help your little brother learn how to ride a bicycle, and he still has not learned.

5. You asked someone for a date and were turned down.

6. You have been working on building a bookcase, but it just doesn't come out right.

7. You wanted to do at least 30 push-ups in a row, but you could only do 23.

8. You have just been told that your grades are not good enough for you to be advanced to the next grade level.

9. You applied for a job and you really wanted it a lot, but you just found out someone else got it.

Skill 10: Responding Constructively to Failure

Name _____ Date _____

> You do not need a partner for this role-play. Follow the steps to help you describe your situation to the group.

Step 1: Ask yourself, "Did I fail?"
Decide if you have failed.

Step 2: Ask yourself, "Why did I fail?"
Think about both the thinking errors and the circumstances that contributed to your failure.

Step 3: Think about what you could do differently next time

Step 4: Decide if you want to try again or get another chance and do better

Step 5: If appropriate, make a plan to try again
Remember how you can do things differently.

Suggested situations for using this skill

1. You failed a test at school.

2. You failed to complete your chores at home.

3. You failed to get the group to do the activity you wanted to do.

4. You spent 3 weeks trying to help your little brother learn how to ride a bicycle, and he still has not learned.

5. You asked someone for a date and were turned down.

6. You have been working on building a bookcase, but it just doesn't come out right.

7. You wanted to do at least 30 push-ups in a row, but you could only do 23.

8. You have just been told that your grades are not good enough for you to be advanced to the next grade level.

9. You applied for a job and you really wanted it a lot, but you just found out someone else got it.

Equipper's Review and Self-Evaluation Form: Social Skills Training

Equipper _____ Date _____

Session/Skill _____ Group _____

In general

☐ yes ☐ no 1. Did group members follow the ground rules (concerning listening, confidentiality, etc.)?

☐ yes ☐ no 2. Were all group members interested and involved?

If no, list the names of uninvolved group members:

_____

_____

_____

☐ yes ☐ no 3. Did you find some constructive value in every serious comment made by a group member?

☐ yes ☐ no 4. Did you maintain a normal voice volume and speak in a respectful rather than threatening or demanding tone?

☐ yes ☐ no 5. Did you maintain a balance between criticism and approval by using the "sandwich" style of constructive criticism (in which a critical comment is preceded and followed by supportive ones)?

☐ yes ☐ no 6. Did you use the "ask, don't tell" intervention as much as possible?

For the session

☐ yes ☐ no 1. Did you read and discuss the Social Skills Role-Playing handout?

☐ yes ☐ no 2. *(After the first session)* Did you review the previous session's activities?

☐ yes ☐ no 3. Which group members tried the skills?

_____

_____

_____

☐ yes ☐ no 4. *(Discuss the skill)* Did the designated group members give "coaching" feedback?

☐ yes ☐ no 5. *(After reading the suggested situations)* Did you encourage group members to think of a suitable situation from their daily lives in which to try the skill?

☐ yes ☐ no 6. *(After all group members tried the skill)* Did group members receive the Social Skills Practice Form?

☐ yes ☐ no 7. Did you encourage group members to try the skill outside the session?

SECTION SEVEN

Social Decision Making

INTRODUCTION

This section provides the materials for equipment meetings pertaining to the development of social decision making skills (i.e., mature moral judgment). You will find that these sessions are usually popular with the youth, even though they are not always comfortable. The social decision making equipment meetings feature the discussion of social "problem situations." Whereas in life there may be a number of legitimate solutions to ethical dilemmas, the EQUIP problem situations typically point toward a single decision that represents responsible thinking and acting in the situation (e.g., not letting a friend steal from the store where you work).

The problem situations are designed to create opportunities for the youths to take the perspectives of others. These opportunities emerge as group members are challenged by peers or sometimes by the equipper. As the equipper, you may be actively challenged at times by many or even all of the group members. Whether challenging or being challenged, you must always stand behind the decision representing responsible thought and action.

The purpose of the social decision making meeting is to facilitate moral-cognitive development, much along the lines this development would naturally take, so the youths will make more mature decisions in social situations. It is your job to facilitate mature moral development by promoting and guiding the group discussion. You can do this by using the indirect "ask, don't tell" technique (see pp. 29–32 of the EQUIP book) or through direct intervention. As you gain experience and the group develops, you should find that direct intervention becomes less necessary.

Facilitation is needed to remedy the sociomoral judgment delay characteristic of youth with a history of antisocial behavior problems. That is, these youths function primarily at the immature stages of moral development and need your prompting and guidance to make more mature decisions in social situations, especially difficult social situations.

FORMAT OF THE SOCIAL DECISION MAKING MEETING

Social decision making meetings have four specific phases. Because these phases flow together naturally, from one to the next, they are not easily identifiable to a person unfamiliar with this type of group. You must continually evaluate what is happening in the group to decide when you will move the group to the next phase of the meeting. Unlike the mutual help meetings and social skills training meetings, there is no announcement or recognition of the start of a new phrase.

Before Beginning

As requested by the busy practitioners with whom we have worked, a Participant Handout is included for each problem situation. These handouts include a description of the problem situation and list several questions for group members to answer. At least a day prior to the meeting, give the group members the handout for the problem situation you will be discussing, and tell them to complete it before the meeting begins. It is important that each youth answer the questions without influence from other youth or the staff. A youth may need help reading the problem situations, but even in this case it is important not to influence the youth's answers. In short, don't let anyone do a youth's assignment for him or her.

You will need an easel pad and a marker for each session (as well as masking tape to display several pages for each session). For the Martian Adviser's Problem Situation, prepare a chart by listing participants' names and drawing and labeling the columns in the way shown (see p. 110). For subsequent problem situations, you should (if at all possible) prepare and analyze a chart that already includes the decision information (see pp. 55–58 of the EQUIP book).

Phase 1: Introducing the Problem Situation

At the beginning of the meeting, ask the questions following the problem situation description. Write down the youths' responses to the questions on the easel pad, as the Martian's Adviser's example shows. At the beginning of the initial (Martian's Adviser's) meeting, ask a group member to read the problem situation aloud. Then ask the questions that follow the problem situation description. Write down the youths' responses to the questions on the easel pad. Mentally note which group members have made right (positive, responsible) decisions (for subsequent meetings, you will have accomplished this chart work beforehand). As you move into the remaining phases, remember that you are an active and energetic member of the group—guide, prompt, and probe as often as needed to develop mature morality, but do not dominate the meeting.

Phase 2: Cultivating Mature Morality

Once the group understands the problem situation, you can proceed to cultivate a group atmosphere of mature morality—that is, of responsible decisions based upon mature moral reasoning (cognitive structures, ways of thinking). It is the group atmosphere of thinking and acting responsibly that will influence the morally immature youths to advance in their sociomoral development.

Call on the group members who had responsible decisions to share their reasons for answering this way. Write those reasons on the easel pad—most of the reasons will be mature. While doing so, you are subtly reinforcing the mature reasoning by calling on those with the responsible decision. You may state your agreement with the mature thinkers to help establish the group atmosphere of mature morality. When you are reasonably sure the atmosphere within the group reflects mature moral reasoning, go on to the next phase.

Phase 3: Remediating Moral Developmental Delay

Once a mature moral tone has been cultivated, you can proceed to take on the problem of developmental delay. Even though an atmosphere of mature moral reasoning may exist for some of the group members, it does not exist for all of them. The developmental delay may be moderate or severe; either way, there is need for remediation. You now call on the group members who did not have the responsible answer to share their reasoning for their decision. Because "can't decide" may partially reflect responsible thinking, call on the undecided participant before calling on the one with the irresponsible decision. Record the reasons on the easel pad. Ask the immature thinkers to react to the majority reasons, and ask mature thinkers to react to the immature (pragmatic, self-centered) reasons. Set the tone for a respectful discussion, then move on to the next phase.

Phase 4: Consolidating Mature Morality

Your goal during this phase is to consolidate mature moral decisions and reasons. Ask if anyone would object to declaring the (positive) majority decision as the group's official decision. (Instead of objecting, some may even ask to change their answer to the majority decision.) If no one objects, suggest that a volunteer circle the group's official decision. If someone does object, then just leave the majority issue alone. (Don't worry—in our experience, objectors tend to join the majority eventually.) Follow the same procedure for the group's most mature reason, which a group member could underline.

It is important for you to be patient. The EQUIP curriculum and the mutual help meetings are constructed to introduce change in a natural, incremental fashion. Your attempts to force change when a youth is not ready to change or is not sufficiently mature in a cognitive sense will only reinforce the "might makes right" and "deals" levels of morality.

STAGES OF MORAL DEVELOPMENT

During the discussion, it is important to keep in mind the stages of moral development. The stages are summarized here; for more detailed information, see pages 46–47 of the EQUIP book.

Stage 1—Power: "Might Makes Right"

Morality is whatever big or powerful people say that you have to do. If you don't get punished for what you did or no one powerful saw it, whatever you did was OK. It is wrong if you do get punished; the punishment is mainly what makes it wrong.

Stage 2—Deals: "You Scratch My Back, I'll Scratch Yours"

Morality is an exchange of favors ("I did this for you, so you'd better do that for me") or of blows (misunderstanding of the Golden Rule as "Do it to others before they do it to you" or "Pay them back if they've done it to you"). The main reason for not stealing, cheating, and so on is that you could get caught.

Stage 3—Mutuality: "Treat Others As You Would Hope They Would Treat You"

In mutual morality, the relationship becomes a value: Trust and mutual caring, although intangible, are real and important. People can really care about other people, can have trust in them, can feel a part of a "we." People try to understand if a friend is acting hostile or selfish.

Stage 4—Systems: "Are You Contributing to Society?"

This morality involves interdependence and cooperation for the sake of society: Society can't make it if people don't respect the rights of others and follow through on commitments. In difficult situations, retaining integrity and self-respect may mean becoming unpopular.

ACTIVITIES AND MATERIALS

For the Problem Situations

1. To prepare for the social decision making meeting, read and study chapter 3 of the EQUIP book.

2. Review the discussion of the indirect, "ask, don't tell" technique on pages 29–32 of the EQUIP book. (At times you will find direct interventions necessary; however, as you gain experience and as the group develops, you should find that you use them less often.)

3. A Participant Handout is included for each of the problem situations. Consult the EQUIP book for the leader notes for each situation. These appear on the following pages of the EQUIP book:

- The Martian's Adviser's Problem Situation (pp. 68–70)
- Jerry's Problem Situation (pp. 71–73)
- Mark's Problem Situation (pp. 74–76)
- Jim's Problem Situation (pp. 77–79)
- Alonzo's Problem Situation (pp. 80–82)
- Sarah's Problem Situation (pp. 83–85)
- George's Problem Situation (pp. 86–88)
- Leon's Problem Situation (pp. 89–90)
- Dave's Problem Situation (pp. 91–93)
- Juan's Problem Situation (pp. 94–96)
- Sam's Problem Situation (pp. 97–98)
- Reggie's Problem Situation (pp. 99–100)
- Antonio's Problem Situation (pp. 101–102)

4. Review the Equipper's Guidelines for the Martian's Adviser's Problem Situation (the first problem situation presented in the social decision making curriculum). Because the social decision making meetings require extensive "ad libbing" by the equipper, we do not provide guidelines for the other problem situations. Use the example of the Martian's Adviser's Problem Situation to give you ideas for presenting the rest of the situations.

5. Arrange to have an easel pad, marker, and masking tape for the sessions; prepare a chart for the particular problem situation similar to the one for the Martian's Adviser's Problem Situation, shown on page 110.

6. Before each meeting, photocopy enough Participant Handouts so every group member may have one.

7. After each meeting, fill out the Equipper's Review and Self-Evaluation Form for social decision making (see pages 125–126 of this guide).

The Martian's Adviser's Problem Situation

A man from Mars has decided to move to another planet. He has narrowed his search down to two planets. Planet A and Planet B. Planet A is a violent and dangerous place to live. People just care about themselves and don't care when they hurt others. Planet B is a safer, more peaceful place. People on Planet B do care about others. They still have fun, but they feel bad if they hurt someone. Planet B people try to make the planet a better place.

You're the Martian's adviser. Which planet should you advise him/her to move to?

Planet A / Planet B / can't decide (circle one)

Overview

The Martian's Adviser's Problem Situation is designed to set the tone for the problem situations that follow. Whereas the subsequent situations stimulate the development of moral judgment, this situation is designed mainly to facilitate the discovery of common values and to foster a cohesive, prosocial group spirit.

Some reasons for choosing Planet B come from the problem situation content:

- There is not as much violence.
- It's more peaceful.
- People get along without fighting, people want to help one another.
- People have fun without hurting others.
- People work to make things better.

Other reasons include the following:

- You can live longer.
- There's less crime.
- There's better listening or communication.
- People are more trustworthy.
- They try to control their anger.
- People apologize.
- Parents spend more time with their kids.

  A few group members may choose Planet A, for the following reasons:

- There'd be lots of drugs and booze and sex.
- Nobody would be sticking their nose in your business.

It is important to emphasize that every group member would like, not only for the Martian but for him- or herself, a world that is positive (safer, more caring, more prosocial, and so on). If some members have chosen and argued for the negative planet, the group should be challenged to refute them. The group, then, is united in the endorsement of these positive and strong values. But the world is what people make it, and the responsibility to act positively and not just talk positively starts with each individual. The same is true for the group. The group should be challenged to make the group a Planet B: "It's up to you."

Probe questions

Record the participants' responses and your responses on the easel pad. Tape the sheets on the wall for ready reference. (See the sample completed chart on the next page.)

Martian's Adviser's Problem Situation			
Name	Planet A	Planet B	Can't decide
Roger		X	
Antoine		X	
Larry	X ⟶	X	
José		X	
Mike		X ⟵	X
Steve	X		
Group decision		XXXXXX	

1. What is the basic thinking error, the basic problem, on Planet A?

The answer, Self-Centered, should be fairly easy to elicit.

2. *(To those favoring Planet A because no one bothers you; if the group needs assistance)* What if someone you did care about—say a parent or brother or sister or close friend—was going to commit suicide? Would you let the person do it and not "bother" him or her? That's what Planet A would be like.

Prompt the group to consider such a world. Typically, Planet A respondents will acquiesce so that the Planet B choice becomes unanimous. Use relabeling to make sure that caring is not stigmatized as weak.

3. Where are the truly strong people? On Planet A or on Planet B?

This question helps apply the "planet" to the group.

4. What kind of group do you want this group to be—Planet A or Planet B, negative or positive? If Planet B is what you want for this group, have you been living up to it? Planet B won't happen unless everyone practices what he or she preaches to make it happen. (*Relabeling again.*) But it's not easy. It takes courage; it takes strength.

Most participants will select the positive Planet B. Sometimes this problem situation will stimulate soul-searching.

5. Who has had a friend or acquaintance die a violent death?

Usually at least a few group members will raise their hands or speak up.

6. What do people say about him or her—what kind of difference did he or she make?

7. What kind of difference will people say you made?

Explain: "It's not too early to start thinking about your life—how you're living it, what kind of difference you want to make. Some of your friends may have said they value a Planet B, but their behavior made things more like Planet A."

8. What about you?

>   Note: The arrows indicate that Larry and Mike changed their decisions after the group discussed their reasons for selecting planet B. During the discussion, mature morality was (a) cultivated (= positive decision supported by mature reasons), (b) remediated (= Larry's and Mike's changes to a positive decision with mature reasons), and (c) consolidated (= group's positive decision, mature reasoning).

After this session, "Planet A" and "Planet B" become part of the group vocabulary:

- A collection of individual self-centered and selfish attitudes characterized by mistrust and disruption is "Planet A."

- A climate of mutual caring and trust characterized by well-equipped help for group members is "Planet B."

These terms provide "handles" for contrasting group atmospheres. Such handles make it easier for youths who are otherwise concrete thinkers to bring to mind hypothetical group weaknesses and ideals.

Session 1: The Martian's Adviser's Problem Situation

Name _____ Date _____

A man from Mars has decided to move to another planet. He has narrowed his search down to two planets. Planet A and Planet B. Planet A is a violent and dangerous place to live. People just care about themselves and don't care when they hurt others. Planet B is a safer, more peaceful place. People on Planet B do care about others. They still have fun, but they feel bad if they hurt someone. Planet B people try to make the planet a better place.

You're the Martian's adviser. Which planet should you advise him/her to move to?

Planet A / Planet B / can't decide (circle one)

Session 2: Jerry's Problem Situation

Name _____ Date _____

Jerry just moved to a new school and was feeling pretty lonely until one day a guy named Bob came up and introduced himself. "Hi, Jerry. My name is Bob. I heard one of the teachers say you're new here. If you're not doing anything after school today, how about coming over to shoot some baskets?" Pretty soon Jerry and Bob were good friends.

One day when Jerry was shooting baskets by himself, the basketball coach saw him and invited him to try out for the team. Jerry made the team, and every day after school he would practice with the rest of the team. After practice, Jerry and his teammates would always go out together to get something to eat and sit around and talk about stuff. On weekends they would sometimes take trips together.

As Jerry spends more time with the team, he sees less and less of Bob, his old friend. One day, Jerry gets a call from Bob. "Say, I was wondering," says Bob, "if you're not too busy on Thursday, my family is having a little birthday party for me. Maybe you could come over for dinner that night." Jerry tells Bob he'll try to come to the party. But during practice on Thursday, everyone tells Jerry about the great place they're all going to after practice.

What should Jerry say or do?

1. Should Jerry go with the team?

    go with team / go to Bob's party / can't decide (circle one)

2. What if Jerry calls Bob from school and says he's sorry, but something has come up and he can't come over after all? Then would it be all right for Jerry to go with the team?

    go with team / go to Bob's party / can't decide (circle one)

3. What if Jerry considers that his teammates may be upset if Jerry doesn't come—that they may start to think Jerry's not such a good friend? Then would it be all right for Jerry to go with the team?

    go with team / go to Bob's party / can't decide (circle one)

4. What if Jerry thinks that, after all, Bob came along and helped Jerry when Jerry was lonely. Then should Jerry go with the team?

    go with team / go to Bob's party / can't decide (circle one)

5. Let's change the situation a bit. Let's say that before Bob asks Jerry to come over, the teammates ask if Jerry will be coming along on Thursday. Jerry says he thinks so. Then Bob asks Jerry. Then what should Jerry do?

    go with team / go to Bob's party / can't decide (circle one)

6. Which is more important: to have one close friend or to have a group of regular friends?

    one close friend / group of regular friends / can't decide (circle one)

7. Let's change the situation a different way. What if Jerry and Bob are not good friends but instead are just acquaintances? Then should Jerry go with the team?

    go with team / go to Bob's party / can't decide (circle one)

Session 2: Mark's Problem Situation

Name _____ Date _____

Mark has been going steady with a girl named Maria for about 2 months. It used to be a lot of fun to be with her, but lately it's been sort of a drag. There are some other girls Mark would like to go out with now. Mark sees Maria coming down the school hallway.

What should Mark say or do?

1. Should Mark avoid the subject with Maria so Maria's feelings aren't hurt?

   should avoid subject / should bring it up / can't decide (circle one)

2. Should Mark make up an excuse, like being too busy to see Maria, as a way of breaking up?

   excuse / no excuse / can't decide (circle one)

3. Should Mark simply start going out with other girls so that Maria will get the message?

   yes / no / can't decide (circle one)

4. How should Mark respond to Maria's feelings?

5. Let's change the situation a bit. What if Mark and Maria have been living together for several years and have two small children? Then should Mark still break up with Maria?

   should break up / no, shouldn't break up / can't decide (circle one)

6. Let's go back to the original situation. This is what happens: Mark does break up with Maria—he lets her know how he feels and starts dating another girl. Maria feels hurt and jealous and thinks about getting even somehow. Should Maria get even?

   yes, should get even / no, shouldn't get even / can't decide (circle one)

7. What if the tables were turned, and Maria did that to Mark?

   yes, should get even / no, shouldn't get even / can't decide (circle one)

Session 3: Jim's Problem Situation

Name _____ Date _____

Jim and Derek are high school friends. Jim, whose birthday is coming up, has mentioned to Derek how great it would be to have a tape deck to listen to music while he goes about his job driving a van. Derek steals a tape deck from a car in the school parking lot and gives it to Jim for his birthday. Jim is appreciative, not realizing the present is stolen.

The next day Jim sees Scott, another friend. Jim knows Scott has a tape deck and is good at electronics. Jim mentions that he got a tape deck for a birthday present and asks Scott to come over to help install it. "Sure," Scott says with a sigh. "You look down, Scott. What's wrong?" Jim asks. Oh, I was ripped off." Scott says. "Oh, boy. What did they get?" Jim asks. "My tape deck," Scott says. Scott starts describing the stolen tape deck.

Later, Jim starts thinking about how odd it is that Scott's tape deck was stolen just at the time Derek gave him one. Jim gets suspicious and calls Derek. Sure enough, Derek confesses that he stole it, and the car he stole it from turns out to be Scott's car!

It's time for Scott to arrive to help Jim install the tape deck. Scott will probably recognize the tape deck as his. Scott is at the door, ringing the doorbell.

What should Jim—the one who got the stolen birthday present from Derek—say or do?

1. Should Jim tell Scott that Derek took Scott's tape deck?

   should tell / shouldn't tell / can't decide (circle one)

2. How good a friend is Derek? Would Jim be able to trust Derek not to steal from him?

   yes, could trust / no, couldn't trust / can't decide (circle one)

3. Derek stole the tape deck for a good cause (Jim's birthday). Does that make it all right for Derek to steal the tape deck?

   yes, all right / no, not all right / can't decide (circle one)

4. What if Derek didn't steal the tape deck from Scott's car? What if instead Derek stole the tape deck from a stranger's car? Then would it be all right for Derek to steal the tape deck for Jim's birthday?

   yes, all right / no, not all right / can't decide (circle one)

Session 4: Alonzo's Problem Situation

Name _____ Date _____

Alonzo is walking along a side street with his friend Rodney. Rodney stops in front of a beautiful new sports car. Rodney looks inside and then says, excitedly, "Look! The keys are still in this thing! Let's see what it can do! Come on, let's go!"

What should Alonzo say or do?

1. Should Alonzo try to persuade Rodney not to steal this car?

   should persuade / should let steal / can't decide (circle one)

2. What if Rodney says to Alonzo that the keys were left in the car, that anyone that careless deserves to get ripped off? Then should Alonzo try to persuade Rodney not to steal the car?

   should persuade / should let steal / can't decide (circle one)

3. What if Rodney says to Alonzo that the car's owner can probably get insurance money to cover most of the loss? Then should Alonzo try to persuade Rodney not to steal the car?

   should persuade / should let steal / can't decide (circle one)

4. What if Rodney tells Alonzo that stealing a car is no big deal—that plenty of his friends do it all the time? Then what should Alonzo do?

   should persuade / should let steal / can't decide (circle one)

5. What if Alonzo knows that Rodney has a wife and child who will suffer if Rodney gets caught, loses his job, and goes to jail? Then should Alonzo try to persuade Rodney not to steal the car?

   should persuade / should let steal / can't decide (circle one)

6. Let's say the car is *your* car. Alonzo is Rodney's friend, but Alonzo is also your friend. Alonzo knows it's your car. Then should Alonzo try to persuade Rodney not to steal the car?

   should persuade / should let steal / can't decide (circle one)

7. In general, how important is it for people not to take things that belong to others?

   very important / important / not important (circle one)

8. Let's say that Alonzo does try to persuade Rodney not to take the car, but Rodney goes ahead and takes it anyway. Alonzo knows Rodney is in bad shape from being high—he could have a serious accident, and someone could get killed. Then what should Alonzo do?

   contact the police / not contact the police / can't decide (circle one)

Session 4: Sarah's Problem Situation

Name _____ Date _____

Sarah works as a clerk in a small grocery store. The store isn't too busy. Orlando, a friend of Sarah's at school, comes over to her cash register and says, "Hey, I've only got a dollar with me. Ring up these cigarettes and a six-pack for a dollar, won't you? The manager's in the back of the store—he'll never know." Sarah likes Orlando, and Orlando has done some favors for her. But Sarah also feels trusted by the manager.

What should Sarah say or do?

1. Should Sarah refuse Orlando, or should Sarah say yes to Orlando's suggestion?

   should refuse/ should say yes / can't decide (circle one)

2. Was it right for Orlando to put Sarah on the spot with his request?

   yes, right / no, not right / can't decide (circle one)

3. What if Sarah feels that the other employees at the store do this for their friends? Then what should Sarah do?

   should refuse / should say yes / can't decide (circle one)

4. What if Sarah feels that the store is making a profit and wouldn't miss a little money? Then what should Sarah do?

   should refuse / should say yes / can't decide (circle one)

5. What if you are the owner of the grocery store where Sarah is working? Then what should Sarah do?

   should refuse / should say yes / can't decide (circle one)

6. What if the store owner has been sending Sarah home early, when business is slow, and Sarah's paycheck has been cut in half? Then what should Sarah do?

   should refuse / should say yes / can't decide (circle one)

7. How important is it to be honest at a store where you work?

   very important / important / not important (circle one)

8. Let's say that Sarah says no. Orlando then just walks out of the store with the cigarettes and the six-pack. Should Sarah tell the manager?

   yes, tell manager / no, keep quiet / can't decide (circle one)

Session 5: George's Problem Situation

Name _____ Date _____

One day George's older brother, Jake, tells him a secret: Jake is selling drugs. George and Jake both know that the kind of drug Jake is selling is highly addictive and causes lung and brain damage. It can even kill people. George asks his brother to stop selling. But the family is poor, and Jake says he is only doing it to help out with the family's money problems. Jake asks his younger brother not to tell anyone.

What should George say or do?

1. Should George promise to keep quiet and not tell on his brother?

   should keep quiet / should tell / can't decide (circle one)

2. What if Jake tells George that selling drugs is no big deal, that plenty of Jake's friends do it all the time? Then what should George do?

   keep quiet / tell / can't decide (circle one)

3. What if George finds out that Jake is selling the drug to 10-year-olds outside a school? Then what should George do?

   keep quiet / tell / can't decide (circle one)

4. What if Jake himself won't be harmed by the drug—he tells George he knows how addictive and harmful the stuff is and never touches it? Then what should George do?

   keep quiet / tell / can't decide (circle one)

5. What if George finds out that Jake isn't using any of the money at all to "help out the family" but instead is spending it on booze and other things for himself? Then what should George do?

   keep quiet / tell / can't decide (circle one)

6. Is it ever right to tell on someone?

   sometimes right / never right / can't decide (circle one)

7. Who's to blame in this situation?

   George (younger brother) / Jake (drug dealer) / other / can't decide (circle one)

8. How important is it for judges to send drug dealers to jail?

   very important / important / not important (circle one)

Session 5: Leon's Problem Situation

Name _____ Date _____

Just after Leon arrived at an institution for boys, he tried to escape. As a result, he was given extra time. It took Leon nearly 4 months to earn the trust of the staff again. He now thinks it is stupid to try to escape. However, Bob, a friend of Leon's, tells Leon he is planning to escape that night. "I've got it all figured out," Bob says. "I'll hit the youth leader on the head with a pipe and take his keys." Bob asks Leon to come along. Leon tries to talk Bob out of it, but Bob won't listen.

What should Leon say or do?

1. Should Leon tell the staff about Bob's plan to escape?

   tell / keep quiet / can't decide (circle one)

2. What if Bob is a pretty violent type of guy and Leon thinks that Bob might seriously injure, maybe even kill, the youth leader? Then what should Leon do?

   tell / keep quiet / can't decide (circle one)

3. What if the youth leader is mean and everyone hates him? Then what should Leon do?

   tell / keep quiet / can't decide (circle one)

4. Is it any of Leon's business what Bob does?

   can be Leon's business / is none of Leon's business / can't decide (circle one)

5. Is it ever right to nark on somebody?

   yes, sometimes right / no, never right / can't decide (circle one)

6. Let's change the situation a bit. Let's say the youth leader is Leon's uncle. Then what should Leon do?

   tell / keep quiet / can't decide (circle one)

7. Let's change the situation a different way. Let's say Bob is Leon's brother. Then what should Leon do?

   tell / keep quiet / can't decide (circle one)

8. Which is the most important?

   not telling on your friend / not letting other people get hurt / minding your own business (circle one)

Session 6: Dave's Problem Situation

Name _____ Date _____

Dave's friend Matt does some dealing on the street. Once in a while, Matt even gives Dave some smoke for free. Now Matt says to Dave, "Listen, man, I've got to deliver some stuff on the south side, but I can't do it myself. How 'bout it—will you take the stuff down there for me in your car? I'll give you some new stuff to try plus 50 dollars besides for just a half-hour's drive. Will you help me out?"

What should Dave say or do?

1. Should Dave agree to deliver the stuff for Matt?

   yes, should deliver / no, shouldn't deliver / can't decide (circle one)

2. What if Dave knows that the stuff Matt wants him to deliver is laced with poison? Should he agree to deliver it?

   yes, should deliver / no, shouldn't deliver / can't decide (circle one)

3. What if Dave knows that his sister, who lives on the south side, might take some of the laced stuff? Then should he agree to deliver it?

   yes, should deliver / no, shouldn't deliver / can't decide (circle one)

4. Should Dave be taking the free stuff from Matt?

   yes, should take it / no, shouldn't take it / can't decide (circle one)

5. What if Matt says that doing drugs is no big deal, that plenty of his friends use drugs all the time? Then should Dave be taking the free drugs?

   yes / no / can't decide (circle one)

6. Let's say that Dave does make the drug delivery. Since Dave is just helping out Matt, he doesn't feel he's doing anything wrong. Should Dave feel he's doing something wrong?

   yes, wrong / no, not wrong / can't decide (circle one)

7. How important is it to stay away from drugs?

   very important / important / not important (circle one)

Session 7: Juan's Problem Situation

Name _____ Date _____

Juan and Phil are roommates at a juvenile institution. They get along well and have become good friends. Phil has confided that he has been getting pretty depressed lately and has managed to get hold of some razor blades. Juan sees where Phil hides the blades. The youth leader, having learned of the razor blades, searches their room but doesn't find them. So the youth leader asks Juan where the razor blades are hidden.

What should Juan say or do?

1. Should Juan cover for Phil, saying he doesn't know anything about any razor blades?

   cover for Phil / tell the leader / can't decide (circle one)

2. What if Phil has told Juan that he plans to cut his wrists with the razor blades that night? Then what should Juan do?

   cover for Phil / tell the leader / can't decide (circle one)

3. Would Phil feel that Juan cared about him if Juan told?

   yes, would feel Juan cared / no, would not feel Juan cared / can't decide (circle one)

4. What if Juan and Phil actually don't get along well and are not friends? What if Phil has been a real pest? Then what should Juan do?

   cover for Phil / tell the leader / can't decide (circle one)

5. What if Juan isn't Phil's roommate but does know about the razor blades and where they are? The youth leader suspects Juan knows something and asks him about the razor blades. Then what should Juan do?

   cover for Phil / tell the leader / can't decide (circle one)

6. How important is it for a juvenile institution to have rules against contraband?

   very important / important / not important (circle one)

7. How important is it to live even when you don't want to?

   very important / important / not important (circle one)

8. Who might be affected (in addition to Phil himself) if Phil were to commit suicide?

Session 8: Sam's Problem Situation

Name _____ Date _____

Sam and his friend John are shopping in a music store. Sam has driven them to the store. John picks up a CD he really likes and slips it into his backpack. With a little sign for Sam to follow, John then walks out of the store. But Sam doesn't see John. Moments later, the security officer and the store owner come up to Sam. The store owner says to the officer, "That's one of the boys who was stealing CDs." The security officer checks Sam's backpack but doesn't find the CD: "OK, you're off the hook, but what's the name of the guy who was with you?" the officer asks Sam. "I'm almost broke because of shoplifters," the owner says. "I can't let him get away with it."

What should Sam say or do?

1. Should Sam keep quiet and refuse to tell the security officer John's name?

   keep quiet / tell / can't decide (circle one)

2. From the store owner's point of view, what should Sam do?

   keep quiet / tell / can't decide (circle one)

3. What if the store owner is a nice guy who sometimes lets kids buy tapes or CDs even if they don't have quite enough money? Then what should Sam do?

   keep quiet / tell / can't decide (circle one)

4. What if the store owner is Sam's father? Then what should Sam do?

   keep quiet / tell / can't decide (circle one)

5. Is it ever right to tell on someone?

   yes, sometimes / no, never / can't decide (circle one)

6. Who's to blame in this situation?

   Sam / John / the store owner / other / can't decide (circle one)

7. How important is it not to shoplift?

   very important / important / not important (circle one)

8. How important is it for store owners to prosecute shoplifters?

   very important / important / not important (circle one)

Session 9: Reggie's Problem Situation

Name _____ Date _____

"Your father is late again," Reggie's mother tells Reggie one night as he sits down to dinner. Reggie knows why. He passed his father's car on the way home from school. It was parked outside the Midtown Bar and Grill. Reggie's mother and father had argued many times about his father's stopping off at the bar on his way home from work. After their last argument, his father had promised he would never do it again. "I wonder why your father is late," Reggie's mother says. Do you think I should trust what he said about not drinking any more? Do you think he stopped off at the bar again?" Reggie's mother asks him.

What should Reggie say or do?

1. Should Reggie cover for his father by lying to his mother?

   yes, should cover / no, should tell the truth / can't decide (circle one)

2. Was it right for Reggie's mother to put Reggie on the spot by asking him a question about his father?

   yes, right / no, wrong / can't decide (circle one)

3. What if Reggie's father drinks a lot when he stops at the bar and then comes home and often beats up on Reggie's mother—sometimes even on Reggie? Then what should Reggie do?

   cover for him / tell the truth / can't decide (circle one)

4. Which is most important for Reggie's decision?

   what's best for himself / what's best for his mom / what's best for his dad / what's best for the family (circle one)

5. In general, how important is it to tell the truth?

   very important / important / not important (circle one)

Session 10: Antonio's Problem Situation

Name _____ Date _____

Antonio is in school taking a math test. Suddenly, the teacher says, "I'm going to leave the room for a few minutes. You are on your honor not to cheat." After the teacher has gone, Ed, Antonio's friend, whispers to him, "Let me see your answers, Antonio."

What should Antonio say or do?

1. Should Antonio let Ed copy his answers?

   yes, let cheat / no, don't let cheat / can't decide (circle one)

2. What if Ed whispers that cheating is no big deal, that he knows plenty of guys who cheat all the time? Then should Antonio let Ed cheat?

   yes, let cheat / no, don't let cheat / can't decide (circle one)

3. What if Antonio knows that Ed is flunking because he doesn't study? Then should Antonio let Ed cheat?

   yes, let cheat / no, don't let cheat / can't decide (circle one)

4. What if *you* were the teacher? Would you want Antonio to let Ed cheat?

   yes, let cheat / no, don't let cheat / can't decide (circle one)

5. Is it possible to have a really close, trusting friendship with someone who has a cheating or lying problem?

   yes, possible / no, not possible / can't decide (circle one)

6. Let's change the situation a little. What if Antonio hardly knows Ed? Then should Antonio let Ed cheat?

   yes, let cheat / no, don't let cheat / can't decide (circle one)

7. In general, how important is it not to cheat?

   very important / important / not important (circle one)

8. Is it right for teachers to punish cheaters?

   yes, right / no, not right / can't decide (circle one)

Equipper's Review and Self-Evaluation Form: Social Decision Making

Equipper _____ Date _____

Session/Problem Situation _____ Group _____

In general

☐ yes ☐ no 1. Did group members follow the ground rules (concerning listening, confidentiality, etc.)?

☐ yes ☐ no 2. Were all group members interested and involved?

If no, list the names of uninvolved group members:

_____

_____

_____

☐ yes ☐ no 3. Did you find some constructive value in every serious comment made by a group member?

☐ yes ☐ no 4. Did you maintain a normal voice volume and speak in a respectful rather than threatening or demanding tone?

☐ yes ☐ no 5. Did you maintain a balance between criticism and approval by using the "sandwich" style of constructive criticism (in which a critical comment is preceded and followed by supportive ones)?

☐ yes ☐ no 6. Did you use the "ask, don't tell" intervention as much as possible?

For the session

In the various phases, did you . . .

Phase 1: Introducing the problem situation

☐ yes ☐ no 1. Make sure the group understood the problem situation (e.g., "Who can tell the group just what Jerry's problem situation is? Why is that a problem?")?

☐ yes ☐ no 2. Relate the problem situation to group members' everyday lives (e.g., "Do problems like this happen? Who has been in a situation like this? Tell the group about it.")?

Phase 2: Cultivating mature morality

☐ yes ☐ no 3. Establish mature morality as the tone for the rest of the meeting (e.g., eliciting and listing on the easel pad reasons for each positive majority decision)?

☐ yes ☐ no 4. Did you support and relabel the "should" as strong (e.g., "Yes, it does take guts to do the right thing")?

Phase 3: Remediating moral developmental delay

☐ yes ☐ no 5. Use more mature group members and their reasons (Phase 2) to challenge the hedonistic or pragmatic arguments of some group members?

☐ yes ☐ no 6. Create role-taking opportunities in other ways as well (e.g., "What would the world be like if everybody did that?"; "How would you feel if you were Bob?")?

Phase 4: Consolidating mature morality

☐ yes ☐ no 7. Make positive decisions and mature reasons unanimous for the group (e.g., "Any strong objections if I circle that decision as the group decision/underline that reason as the group's number one reason?")?

☐ yes ☐ no 8. Praise the group for its positive decisions and mature reasons (e.g., "I'm really pleased that the group was able to make so many good, strong decisions and back them up with good, strong reasons"; "Would the group like to tape this sheet onto the wall?")?

Post-meeting

☐ yes ☐ no 9. Did you make notes regarding the session and individual group members?

FINAL EQUIPMENT MEETING

Up or Down?

This meeting gives group members a chance to review the ideas that have been presented during the preceding equipment meetings and to consolidate their learning. Participants can use the meeting to strengthen their commitment to a positive, constructive life, characterized by respect for others as well as for self. This is in contrast to a negative, destructive life with little regard for others' feelings or experience. In the meeting, *Up* equals positive or responsible. *Down* equals negative or irresponsible.

The Up or Down? Participant Handout is used at the conclusion of the equipment meetings. Besides helping the group to consolidate their learning, this activity also gives you helpful information for deciding when you should begin a new cycle of equipment meetings. If there has been a large turnover in the group, and many participants did not participate in many of the meetings, then it is fairly obvious that new equipment meetings should be scheduled right away. If this is not the case and you are unsure, the following questions are useful:

- Did several group members have difficulty identifying the correct responses on the Up or Down handout? If so, it would be good to begin the meetings fairly soon.

- Did the group give correct responses and have a positive discussion? In that case, it may be beneficial to delay the next round of equipment meetings for a week or so.

Repeating the equipment meeting cycle provides the group with the opportunity to perfect their skills. "Drill" is just as important to the success of these skills as it is to the skills athletes are required to practice, then practice repeatedly, until they are automatic.

Up or Down?

The Participant Handout may be distributed before or during the session. Either way, participants should be reminded not to share their answers.

Overview of activities

- Review and opportunity to answer questions about thoughts, skills, and behaviors spanning all three EQUIP curriculum components
- Provision of motivational comments
- Test of knowledge relating to curriculum content
- Encouragement to use concepts and skills learned in equipment meetings to help others and oneself

Materials

- Participant Handout: Up or Down?

Procedure

1. Introduce the meeting by letting group members know that this activity provides a review of what has been discussed during the equipment meetings. Explain that the concept "up or down" can be used to describe thoughts, skills, or behaviors: *Up* equals positive or responsible. *Down* equals negative or irresponsible.

2. Tell group members that they have been learning about two kinds of lives:

   The Planet A life involves victimizing, which is destructive and in which you hurt other people and yourself. This life pulls everyone *Down!*

   The Planet B life is constructive and responsible. It involves helping other people and yourself. This life lifts everyone *Up!*

3. Let participants know that each person is responsible for choosing the type of life he or she will live. The truly strong people choose to live a positive and constructive life that lifts them up and gains them respect from their family, friends, and other people.

4. Lead the group through the list given on the Participant Handout, encouraging discussion of each item. Emphasize the areas that the group or an individual may have struggled with during previous sessions. Verbally reward the group and/or individuals for their strength and willingness to change.

5. Share with the group that this cycle of equipment meetings is now complete. However, it is very important for them to continue to practice the things they have learned. Let them know when the next cycle of equipment meetings will begin.

Up or Down?

Check the correct response. Up *is responsible.* Down *is irresponsible.*

Thought, skill, or behavior	Up?	Down?
1. Planet A	☐	☐
2. Noticing an early warning sign of anger	☐	☐
3. Constructively expressing a complaint	☐	☐
4. Apologizing if you're partly responsible for a problem	☐	☐
5. Stealing and thinking it's OK because you didn't steal from anyone you knew	☐	☐
6. Caring for someone sad or upset	☐	☐
7. Using put-downs and threats	☐	☐
8. Stealing a car with the excuse that the owner left the keys in the car	☐	☐
9. Taking deep breaths when angry	☐	☐
10. Making a Self-Centered thinking error	☐	☐
11. Doing it to others before they do it to you	☐	☐
12. Doing it for others only if they will do it for you	☐	☐
13. Preparing for a stressful conversation	☐	☐
14. Selling harmful drugs	☐	☐
15. Giving in to peer pressure to hurt someone	☐	☐
16. Suggesting a responsible alternative to a negative act your friends want you to do	☐	☐
17. Responding constructively to others' anger	☐	☐
18. Thinking ahead to consequences	☐	☐
19. Using self-evaluation	☐	☐
20. Using "I" statements	☐	☐
21. Keeping out of fights	☐	☐
22. Victimizing others and using the excuse that you were a victim	☐	☐
23. Delivering drugs for a friend	☐	☐
24. Blaming the victim	☐	☐
25. Thinking whether the person is right when you are accused of something	☐	☐
26. Expressing care and appreciation	☐	☐
27. Not telling on a suicidal friend	☐	☐
28. Thinking like a victimizer	☐	☐
29. Covering for your shoplifting friend	☐	☐
30. Responding constructively to failure	☐	☐
31. Helping a friend cheat	☐	☐
32. Showing how you would want to be treated by the way you treat others	☐	☐
33. Planet B	☐	☐

References

Ahlborn, H. H. (1986). *Dilemma session intervention with adult female offenders: Behavioral and attitudinal correlates.* Unpublished manuscript, Ohio Department of Rehabilitation and Correction. Columbus.

Colby, A., & Speicher, B. (1973). *Dilemmas for applied use.* Unpublished manuscript, Harvard University, Cambridge, MA.

Dahlberg, L. L., Toal, S. B., & Behrens, C. B. (1998). *Measuring violence-related attitudes, beliefs, and behaviors among youths: A compendium of assessment tools.* Atlanta: Centers for Disease Control and Prevention.

Feindler, E. L., & Ecton, R. R. (1986). *Adolescent anger control: Cognitive-behavioral techniques.* New York: Pergamon.

Freedman, B. J. (1974). *An analysis of social behavioral skill deficits in delinquent and nondelinquent adolescent boys.* Unpublished doctoral dissertation, University of Wisconsin, Madison.

Gibbs, J. C., Barriga, A. Q., & Potter, G. B. (2001). *How I Think (HIT) Questionnaire.* Champaign, IL: Research Press.

Gibbs, J. C., Barriga, A. Q., Potter, G. B., & Liau, A. K. (2001). *How I Think (HIT) Questionnaire manual.* Champaign, IL: Research Press.

Gibbs, J. C., Basinger, K. S., & Fuller, D. (1992). *Moral maturity: Measuring the development of sociomoral reflection.* Hillsdale, NJ: Erlbaum.

Gibbs, J. C., Potter, G. B., & Goldstein, A. P. (1995). *The EQUIP program: Teaching youth to think and act responsibly through a peer-helping approach.* Champaign, IL: Research Press.

Goldstein, A P., Glick, B., & Gibbs, J. C. (1998). *Aggression Replacement Training: A comprehensive intervention for aggressive youth* (rev. ed.). Champaign, IL: Research Press.

Goldstein, A. P., & McGinnis, E. (1997). *Skillstreaming the adolescent: New strategies and perspectives for teaching social skills.* Champaign, IL: Research Press.

Horn, M., Shively, R., & Gibbs, J. C. (2001). *EQUIPPED for life* (game). Champaign, IL: Research Press.

McGinnis, E., & Goldstein, A. P. (1997). *Skillstreaming the elementary school child: New strategies and perspectives for teaching social skills* (rev. ed.). Champaign, IL: Research Press.

Meyers, D. W. (1982). *Moral dilemmas at Scioto Village.* Unpublished manuscript, Ohio Department of Youth Services, Columbus.

Yochelson, S., & Samenow, S. E. (1977). *The criminal personality: Vol. 3. The drug user.* Northvale, NJ: Jason Aronson.

About the Authors

Granville Bud Potter, M.Ed. (Bowling Green State University, 1975), is currently self-employed as a consultant to correctional and educational agencies. He retired from the Ohio Department of Youth Services in 1998 after 30 years of experience within institutions and the parole divisions. While self-employed, he has worked with agencies in 21 of the United States and 2 states in Australia. He is the immediate Past-President of the Ohio Correctional and Court Services Association. Much of his professional experience has involved the use of a peer-group modality.

John C. Gibbs, Ph.D., is professor of psychology at The Ohio State University. His work has concerned developmental theory, assessment of social cognition and moral judgment development, and interventions with conduct-disordered adolescents. He has coauthored numerous books, including *The Measurement of Moral Judgment* (Vol. 2); *Moral Maturity: Measuring the Development of Sociomoral Reflection; The EQUIP Program: Teaching Youth to Think and Act Responsibly through a Peer-Helping Approach*, and the revised edition of *Aggression Replacement Training: A Comprehensive Intervention for Aggressive Youth*.

Arnold P. Goldstein, Ph.D., joined the clinical psychology section of Syracuse University's Psychology Department in 1963 and both taught there and directed its Psychotherapy Center until 1980. In 1981, he founded the Center for Research on Aggression, which he currently directs. He joined Syracuse University's Division of Special Education in 1985 and in 1990 helped organize and codirect the New York State Taskforce on Juvenile Gangs. Dr. Goldstein has a career-long interest in difficult-to-reach clients. Since 1980, his main research and psychoeducational focus has been youth violence. Among Dr. Goldstein's many books are *Delinquents on Delinquency; The Gang Intervention Handbook;* and the recently revised editions of *Skillstreaming the Adolescent: New Strategies and Perspectives for Teaching Prosocial Skills, Aggression Replacement Training: A Comprehensive Intervention for Aggressive Youth,* and *The Prepare Curriculum: Teaching Prosocial Competencies*.